For the Love of
the BOSTON
Red Sox

Saul Wisnia

WEST
SIDE
PUBLISHING

Saul Wisnia has authored numerous books, such as *Chicago Cubs: Yesterday & Today™*, *Best of Baseball*, *Baseball's Prime Time Stars*, and (with Paul Adomites) *Babe Ruth: His Life and Times*. A former sports and feature correspondent for the *Washington Post*, he has contributed to publications including *Red Sox Magazine* and *Sports Illustrated* and is active with both the Society of American Baseball Research and the Boston Braves Historical Association. His favorite "home team" includes wife Michelle, son Jason, and daughter Rachel.

Factual verification by Betsy Rossen Elliot

Excerpt (page 73) "There's nothing in the world like the fatalism of the Red Sox fans…" reprinted from *The Vermont Guardian*, April 12, 2007. Used by permission of the publisher.

Excerpt (page 241) reprinted from *The Boston Globe*, September 12, 1979. Copyright © Globe Newspaper Company.

Front cover: **Getty Images** (top left, right & bottom left); **PIL Collection** (left center)

Back cover: **AP Images** (right); **PIL Collection** (left)

AP Images: contents, 9, 28, 39, 49, 53 (left), 63, 64, 67, 71, 72 (left), 81, 86, 90, 100, 103, 108, 109, 113, 114, 115, 117, 129 (left), 137, 146, 159, 169, 179, 182, 183, 187 (left), 188, 197, 205, 207, 209, 212, 214, 223, 227, 237, 241, 247 (center), 251, 255 (right), 258, 264, 268, 271, 277, 285; **Baseball Antiquities, Ltd., Boston, MA, www.baseballantiquities.com:** 259; **Boston Public Library, Print Department:** 6, 7, 16, 17, 18, 69, 88, 144, 145, 167, 180 (center), 195; Leslie Jones, 78, 196; **©Corbis:** Bettmann, 105, 129 (right), 132, 139, 151, 171, 175, 218, 233, 248, 253, 255 (top), 270; Matt Campbell/epa, 234, 235; Rick Friedman, 98, 125; CJ Gunther/epa, 283; Reuters, 55, 221 (left); Jessica Rinaldi/Reuters, 46 (right); Brian Snyder/Reuters, 75; Ray Stubblebine/Reuters, 211; Underwood & Underwood, 68, 91 (right), 168; **Dana-Farber Cancer Institute:** 278, 279; **Getty Images:** 5, 14, 23, 32, 37, 44, 45, 61 (top), 70, 97, 102, 104, 126, 135, 141, 147, 154, 156, 160, 189, 216, 222, 230, 239, 250, 255 (left), 260, 262 (left), 273, 281; AFP, 89, 121, 133; Diamond Images, 131, 274; Focus on Sport, 101, 143, 221 (right), 229; MLB Photos, 58, 79 (right), 83, 94, 107, 118, 165, 228; *Sports Illustrated*, 46 (left), 72 (right), 203, 246, 262 (right); Time Life Pictures, 123, 208, 221 (center), 242, 244, 245; **Richard Johnson Collection:** 252, 254, 282; **Paul Keleher:** 174; **Library of Congress:** 192; **Michael Naselroad:** 201; **National Baseball Hall of Fame Library, Cooperstown, N.Y.:** 11, 29 (left), 40, 57, 215; **PhotoDisc:** 25, 29 (right), 36, 53 (right), 157, 180 (left), 200, 226 (left); **PIL Collection:** title page, contents, 8, 10, 12, 24, 26, 27, 30, 31, 34, 38, 42, 43, 50, 52, 65, 82, 84, 85, 110, 116, 130, 134, 138, 150, 163, 176, 187 (right), 198, 213, 217, 224, 226 (right), 267, 284 (right); **Mark Rucker Collection, Transcendental Graphics:** 59, 61 (bottom), 91 (left), 148, 152, 172, 231; **Shutterstock:** 13, 33, 66, 76, 77, 79 (left), 122, 173, 181, 184–185, 194, 247 (top); **WireImage:** 99, 155, 191

Photography: PDR Productions, Inc.

West Side Publishing is a division of Publications International, Ltd.

Louis Weber, CEO
Publications International, Ltd.
7373 North Cicero Avenue
Lincolnwood, Illinois 60712

Permission is never granted for commercial purposes.

ISBN-13: 978-1-4127-1600-0
ISBN-10: 1-4127-1600-4

Manufactured in China.

8 7 6 5 4 3 2 1

Library of Congress Control Number: 2008931655

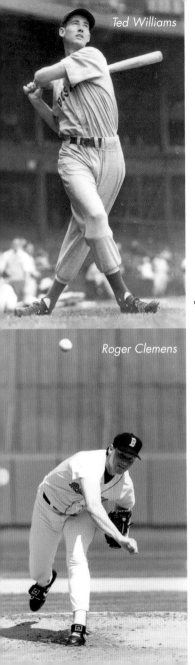

Ted Williams

Roger Clemens

CONTENTS

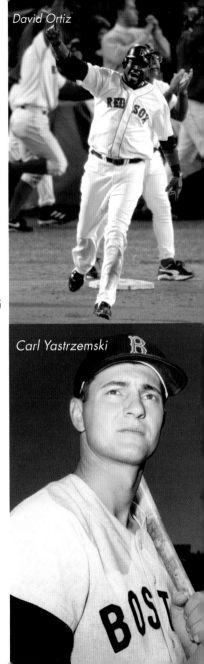

David Ortiz

Carl Yastrzemski

CHAPTER ONE

A NEW ENGLAND INSTITUTION

> "*The Yankees belong to George Steinbrenner and the Dodgers belong to Manifest Destiny, but the Red Sox, more than any other team, belong to the fans.*"

—STEVE WULF, *SPORTS ILLUSTRATED*, 1981

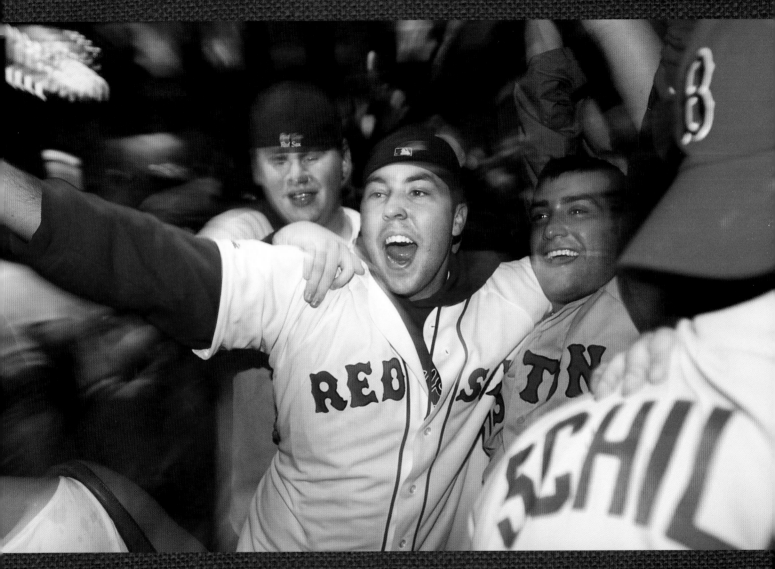

NEW LEAGUE, NEW TEAM

Although Boston had baseball's most successful team in the early days of the National League, times were changing for the circuit and the city as the 20th century dawned. Players throughout the NL were disgruntled by a league structure that allowed powerful owners to keep salaries low and employ a "reserve clause" that prevented athletes from playing where they wanted. Drinking, gambling, and fighting were commonplace at games, and attendance and profits waned.

Ban Johnson, president of a successful minor league, decided the time was right to offer an alternative. He sought out interested owners and cities—many of them already homes to NL franchises—and on January 28, 1901, he officially established baseball's second major league: the American League.

Looking to make a powerful statement with a Boston team, Johnson helped secure land for a new American League ballpark directly across the railroad tracks from the South End Grounds, home of the city's NL club. When it opened on May 8,

1901, the Huntington Avenue Grounds *(opposite)* offered fans 25-cent tickets—half the going rate for National League games—and a quality product. Some of the stars lured from the Boston Nationals by higher salaries were third baseman/captain Jimmy Collins, first baseman Buck Freeman, and pitching ace Ted Lewis. Many fans quickly switched their allegiances to the Boston "Americans" and were rewarded with a championship two years later.

1901 Boston Americans

Carl Yastrzemski

Red Sox Named American League Most Valuable Player

*Tris Speaker, CF........................ 1912

Jimmie Foxx, 1B........................ 1938

Ted Williams, LF........................ 1946

Ted Williams, LF........................ 1949

Jackie Jensen, RF 1958

Carl Yastrzemski, LF.................. 1967

Fred Lynn, CF............................ 1975

Jim Rice, LF/DH 1978

Roger Clemens, P...................... 1986

Mo Vaughn, 1B.......................... 1995

Dustin Pedroia, 2B.................... 2008

*Then called the Chalmers Award

RED-HOT ROOKIES

Ted Williams, 1939

Sent down to the minors during spring training of 1938, a brash young Ted Williams told Boston's snickering starting outfielders that he'd soon be back—and making more than the three of them combined. A year later, "The Kid" started living up to his word.

Williams, the most fantastic rookie hitter Red Sox fans had ever seen, doubled off Yankee Hall of Famer Red Ruffing in his first game, and by season's end he'd gotten to just about every other American League pitcher as well. The sweet-swinging lefty finished seventh in the American League in batting, fourth in slugging, second in runs, and first in runs batted in—setting a rookie RBI mark that was still intact 70 years later.

ROOKIE YEAR TOTALS											
BA	G	AB	R	H	2B	3B	HR	RBI	SB	OBP	SLG
.327	149	565	131	185	44	11	31	145	2	.436	.609

DICK WILLIAMS, THE SOX, AND THE
"Impossible Dream"

In an era when contending teams and sellout crowds are the norm at Fenway, it's easy to forget there was a time when the Red Sox were not a dominant force in baseball and New England. It's also easy to pinpoint the year everything changed: 1967.

The Sox had been floundering, finishing under .500 from 1959 through '66 and ending in seventh place or lower since '62. Attendance had dropped, and the team possessed a reputation as a "country club" of prima donnas.

However, something different was in the offing. New general manager Dick O'Connell was developing strong young players, but the biggest change came when former Sox utility man Dick Williams was hired as manager in September 1966. Just 37, sporting a crew cut and drill sergeant attitude to match, he boldly predicted the Sox—coming off a ninth-place, 72–90 season—would "win more than we lose" in 1967.

Fans thought Williams overconfident, but his club stayed around .500 into July and then put together a 10-game winning streak that turned New Englanders into believers. Carl Yastrzemski emerged as a superstar—excelling at all phases of the game en route to a Triple Crown/MVP season. Other Sox standouts included George Scott (1B), Rico Petrocelli (SS), and rookies Mike Andrews (2B) and Reggie Smith (CF). Jose Santiago, John Wyatt, and Cy Young Award–winner Jim Lonborg anchored the pitching staff. Veteran pickups Elston Howard, Gary Bell, and Jerry Adair all played key roles, and sportswriters took to calling Boston's pennant charge the "Impossible Dream"—in reference to the hit song from Broadway's *Man of La Mancha*—inspiring a record album (*above*) along the way.

These ballplayers were young, likable, and more racially diverse than any Sox team in history—a per-

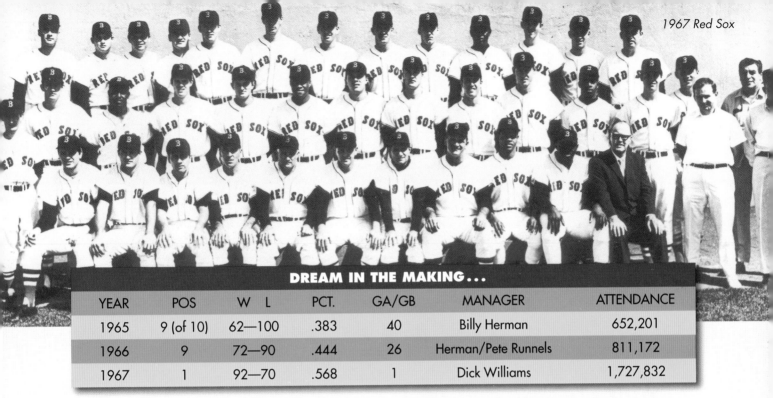

DREAM IN THE MAKING...

YEAR	POS	W—L	PCT.	GA/GB	MANAGER	ATTENDANCE
1965	9 (of 10)	62—100	.383	40	Billy Herman	652,201
1966	9	72—90	.444	26	Herman/Pete Runnels	811,172
1967	1	92—70	.568	1	Dick Williams	1,727,832

fect club to bridge several generations of fans during the Summer of Love. And as summer turned to fall and the first-place Minnesota Twins arrived at Fenway for two season-ending games, the Sox were also one of four teams still bunched at the top of the AL standings. Boston needed to win twice to have a pennant shot; they took the opener 6–4 behind Santiago—with Yaz hitting his 44th homer—but they trailed 2–0 half-way through the finale. Then Lonborg shocked everyone by bunting for a single to lead off the fifth, and before the Twins knew what hit them, the Sox had scored five runs. Lonnie thwarted a late Twins come-back and, after Petrocelli caught the final out, he was carried off on the shoulders of his teammates. Later, after hearing the Detroit Tigers lose on the radio, the Sox knew they were World Series–bound.

CARROLL HARDY
Outfield

Boston
Red Sox

Only One...

Only one man ever pinch-hit for Ted Williams during his four-decade career: Carroll Hardy on September 20, 1960. Just a week before his 2,292nd and final game, Williams fouled a ball off his foot while batting against the Orioles. After Williams limped off the field, Hardy came in, hit into a double play, and punched his ticket to trivia immortality. Interestingly, Carroll also pinch-hit for Carl Yastrzemski the next year—not bad for a guy with a .225 lifetime average.

A Lineup of Massachusetts-born Red Sox

Pitcher: **Bill Monbouquette** of Medford excelled from 1958 to '65, logging a 17-strikeout game, a no-hitter, and (in '63) a 20-win season.

Relief Pitcher: Dalton's own **Jeff Reardon** had 40 saves for the Sox in 1991.

Catcher: **Rich Gedman** of Worcester was an All-Star in 1985 and '86 for Boston.

First Base: Slick-fielding, .300-hitting **Stuffy McInnis** of Gloucester helped the 1918 Sox to a championship.

Second Base: Fan favorite **Jerry Remy** of Somerset was a speedy No. 2 hitter and steady double-play man with Boston from 1978 to '84.

Shortstop: **Hal Janvrin** of Haverhill was a good glove at short and third for the 1915–16 champs.

Third Base: Boston boy **Eddie Pellagrini** homered in his first big-league at-bat in 1946.

Right Field: Revere native **Tony Conigliaro** was a slugging sensation from 1964 to 1970, but injuries cut his career short.

Center Field: **John "Shano" Collins** of Charlestown was one of the few bright lights on dismal 1921–24 Red Sox teams.

Left Field: **Tommy Dowd** of Holyoke was the Boston Americans' first left fielder in 1901, stealing 33 bases and scoring 104 runs.

Designated Hitter: **Harry Agganis,** the "Golden Greek" from Lynn, hit .313 in '55 before his death from a pulmonary embolism at age 26.

Utility: Framingham's **Lou Merloni** played every position but pitcher and catcher with the Sox from 1998 to 2003.

Manager: **Joe Morgan** of Walpole won AL East division titles in 1988 and '90.

PUDGE PERFORMS

After 30-plus years of highlight films, the image most people have of Carlton Fisk is that iconic clip showing the catcher frantically waving his home run fair to win Game 6 of the 1975 World Series. But it was Fisk's everyday labors as a tough-nosed handler of pitchers and a team leader that earned this native New Englander the adoration of Red Sox fans during the '70s.

Raised in Charlestown, New Hampshire, Fisk was a chubby kid (hence his career-long nickname of Pudge) and a superb athlete who went to the University of New Hampshire on a basketball scholarship. In January 1967, however, the Red Sox surprised the catcher by making him their first-round pick, and by September '69 he was up briefly with Boston. Even after steady improvement in two more minor-league seasons, nobody expected what was to come. Fisk's terrific rookie year in '72 included 22 homers, a league-leading nine triples, and a Gold Glove as he displayed the poise of a veteran and instantly became a clubhouse force.

The unanimous AL Rookie of the Year, Fisk hit 26 homers in his sophomore campaign of '73 but endured a horrific second-half slump. His resolve was further tested the next June when he tore ligaments in his left knee during a home-plate collision. After a grueling yearlong rehabilitation, extended by a broken forearm in spring training of 1975, he returned to hit .331 in that season's second half. The Red Sox captured the AL East, and Fisk thrived in the '75 playoffs—hitting clutch homers, arguing with umpires, and urging his pitchers on against heavily favored Oakland and Cincinnati. Boston came up one run short of a World Series title, but Pudge emerged a hero.

Following a teamwide slump in 1976, the Sox returned to contending status in 1977 as Fisk had an outstanding season: .315 average, 26 homers, 102 RBI, and 106 runs. His defense and game-calling remained impeccable, and with hard-fought divisional races against the Yankees that year and in '78, manager Don Zimmer seldom rested him. Pudge played 309 of the club's 325 games those two seasons, 305 at catcher, but Boston came up short twice.

Coming into his early 30s, often the death knell for catchers, Fisk battled injuries in 1979 and 1980 but still earned his seventh All-Star selection. The unnecessary contract snafu that led to his signing a lucrative free-agent deal with the White Sox in 1981 was heartbreaking for Boston fans, all the more so when the Hall of Famer played an amazing 13 more seasons and hit 214 of his 376 career homers for Chicago.

Stellar Stat: How valuable was Fisk to the Red Sox? In 1980 Boston went 68–44 with him catching and 15–33 when others donned the mask.

RED SOX TOTALS (1969, 1971–80)											
BA	G	AB	R	H	2B	3B	HR	RBI	SB	OBP	SLG
.284	1,078	3,860	627	1,097	207	33	162	568	61	.356	.481
MAJOR LEAGUE TOTALS (1969, 1971–93)											
BA	G	AB	R	H	2B	3B	HR	RBI	SB	OBP	SLG
.269	2,499	8,756	1,276	2,356	421	47	376	1,330	128	.341	.457

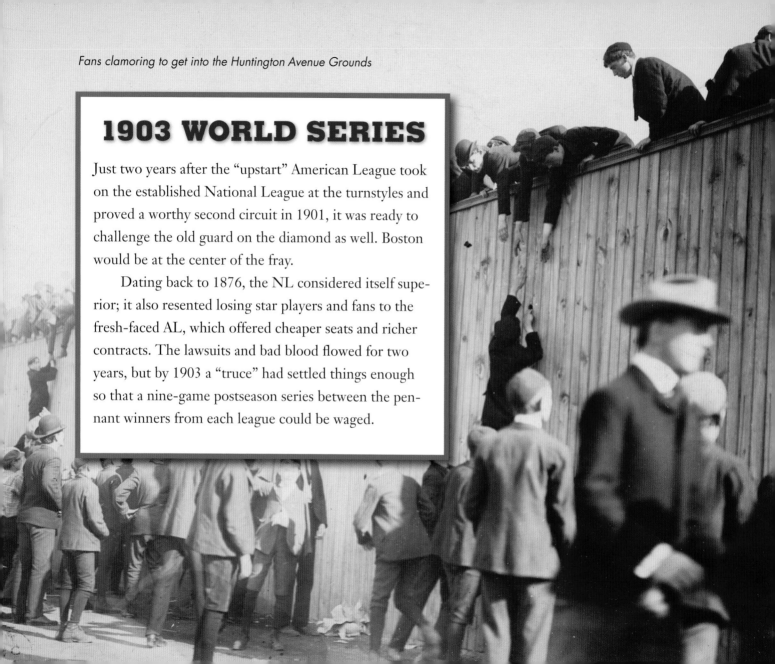

Fans clamoring to get into the Huntington Avenue Grounds

1903 WORLD SERIES

Just two years after the "upstart" American League took on the established National League at the turnstyles and proved a worthy second circuit in 1901, it was ready to challenge the old guard on the diamond as well. Boston would be at the center of the fray.

Dating back to 1876, the NL considered itself superior; it also resented losing star players and fans to the fresh-faced AL, which offered cheaper seats and richer contracts. The lawsuits and bad blood flowed for two years, but by 1903 a "truce" had settled things enough so that a nine-game postseason series between the pennant winners from each league could be waged.

1903 Boston Americans, with Cy Young (standing)

The Boston Americans hosted the first-ever modern World Series game at the Huntington Avenue Grounds but lost that contest and three of the first four to shortstop legend Honus Wagner's Pittsburgh Pirates. As huge crowds in both cities threatened to turn every game into a riot, pitching aces Bill Dinneen and Cy Young led Boston back. The Game 8 finale featured a four-hitter by Dinneen, with second baseman Hobe Ferriss driving in all of Boston's runs in a 3-0 victory. The American Leaguers were upstarts no more.

Classic Kernel: Bill Dinneen later became an American League umpire. He served 29 years in this post and worked 45 games over eight World Series.

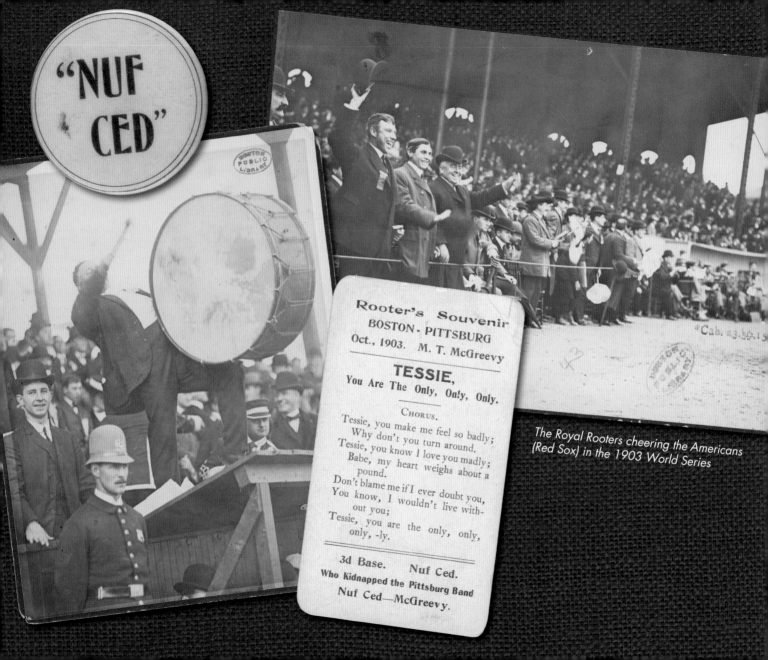

"NUF CED"

Rooter's Souvenir
BOSTON - PITTSBURG
Oct., 1903. M. T. McGreevy

TESSIE,
You Are The Only, Only, Only.

CHORUS.

Tessie, you make me feel so badly;
Why don't you turn around.
Tessie, you know I love you madly;
Babe, my heart weighs about a
pound.
Don't blame me if I ever doubt you,
You know, I wouldn't live with-
out you;
Tessie, you are the only, only,
only, -ly.

3d Base.   Nuf Ced.
Who Kidnapped the Pittsburg Band
Nuf Ced—McGreevy.

The Royal Rooters cheering the Americans (Red Sox) in the 1903 World Series

"TESSIE" AND THE ROYAL ROOTERS

Although the Red Sox can trace their roots to 1901 and the start of the American League, the team's passionate fan base has a pedigree that extends back even further.

The Boston Nationals, founding fathers of the National League in 1876 and still playing today as the Atlanta Braves, were the class of the early NL with eight pennants before the 20th century—including five in the 1890s alone. The most ardent of their fans were a 250-person contingent dubbed "The Royal Rooters," who cheered and sang together at games and drank with their ballplayer heroes afterward. Their bar of choice was 3rd Base Saloon ("Your last stop on the way home"), filled with baseball memorabilia and owned by Rooters leader Michael "Nuf-Ced" McGreevy.

When the American League came along with its cheaper ticket prices and raided the Nationals of their best players, McGreevy's crew and bar largely switched allegiances. And when the Americans (Red Sox) dueled the Pirates in the 1903 World Series, the Rooters descended on Pittsburgh by train with their megaphones, drums, and banners to heckle the home team with the popular song "Tessie"—enhanced by new lyrics written to defame the Pirates lineup. Even Pittsburgh players later admitted the refrain got under their skin and may have played a role in Boston winning the Series.

The Rooters kept up their act through Boston's successful fall classic sojourns of 1912, '15, '16, and '18, but the group aged and fell apart with the team after that. Then, in 2004, Red Sox Public Relations Director Dr. Charles Steinberg had an intriguing idea: Maybe if the Sox brought back the song "Tessie," they could win another World Series. Boston rock band the Dropkick Murphys was asked to do the honors, and we all know what happened next.

Needless to say, "Tessie" remains a popular Fenway ballad—it is played after each Sox victory.

KNUCKLE UP

There are things people come to expect living in Boston: unpredictable weather, traffic jams, and "quality innings" from Tim Wakefield.

Salvaged from the scrap heap in 1995—at which point he started his Red Sox career 14–1—the ageless knuckleballer has slowly moved up the team's victory charts to the point where the only pitchers now ahead of him are named Young and Clemens. He's never won 20 games, but his steady annual production into his 40s has proven invaluable. So has his emergency relief help, which in 1999 resulted in 15 saves. And when it comes to teammates, they don't come any better.

WAKE-UP CALL

Innings (1995–2010): 195.1, 211.2, 201.1, 216.0, 140.0, 159.1, 168.2, 163.1, 202.1, 188.1, 225.1, 140.0, 189.0, 181.0, 129.2, 140.0; **Total: 2,851.1**

Wins (1995–2010): 16, 14, 12, 17, 6, 6, 9, 11, 11, 12, 16, 7, 17, 10, 11, 4; **Total: 179**

Stellar Stat: Wakefield's 16 years of continuous service through 2010 are a record for Red Sox pitchers. In 2009 at age 42, he was the oldest first-time All-Star since Satchel Paige.

SOX STUMPERS: *The 1940s and '50s*

1. In which year did Ted Williams win his first MVP Award: 1941, when he hit .406; or 1942, when he won his first Triple Crown?

2. Who began his pitching career 8–0 for the 1945 Red Sox, en route to a 21–10 rookie season?

3. Which center fielder made a weak relay throw to Johnny Pesky during Enos Slaughter's "mad dash" to win the 1946 World Series?

4. This versatile right-hander had 23 wins for Boston in 1949 and 27 saves four years later. Who is he?

5. Which outfield teammate of Ted Williams played in both the World Series and the Rose Bowl before joining the Red Sox?

6. Who hit 13 home runs in 26 games for Boston in July 1951 but topped 20 homers in a season just once?

7. Who was the Red Sox' first Gold Glove winner, earning the award at third base in 1957?

8. Which 1950s Red Sox All-Star catcher later owned a successful bowling alley in Boston?

Answers

1. Neither. Incredibly, Ted finished second in voting both years—to Yankees Joe DiMaggio in 1941 and Joe Gordon in '42.

2. Boo Ferriss, who followed that up with a 25–6 slate in 1946.

3. Leon Culberson, who had taken over for injured Dom DiMaggio in the eighth.

4. Ellis Kinder, who had 86 wins and 91 saves in his Red Sox career.

5. Jackie Jensen, who played in the 1950 World Series with the Yankees and the 1949 Rose Bowl as an All-American halfback for California.

6. Clyde Vollmer; "Dutch the Clutch" had 40 RBI that month and won numerous games with big hits, including a 16th-inning grand slam.

7. Frank Malzone, who won the honor each year from 1957 to '59.

8. Sammy White—whose "Sammy White's Brighton Bowl" was a popular hangout for Sox fans for decades.

BOOOOOOOOOONE

This was the worst. You can take your Bucky Dents and Bill Buckners, your Denny Galehouses and Joe Morgans and Enos Slaughters, too. The 2003 Red Sox were not only poised to reach the World Series, they were going to do so by beating the Yankees in Game 7 of the AL Championship Series at Yankee Stadium. But that was until Grady Little's brain locked and Aaron Boone's bat mucked up the works.

The two ancient rivals started aces Roger Clemens and Pedro Martinez, but Boston blew out the Rocket early and had a 4–2 lead when Martinez pointed skyward after the seventh inning—a regular ritual for noting his day's work was done. Pedro had allowed three hits in the seventh, including a home run, and had thrown exactly 100 pitches. Even Little Leaguers knew that this was when the fragile phenom lost his edge, but Little apparently forgot. He left a gassed Martinez out there in the eighth until the Yanks had tied the game 5–5, and after three more tense frames they untied it when Boone hit Tim Wakefield's first pitch of the 11th into the seats down the left-field line. Wake need not worry about being the goat, however; there would be only one for this game—his soon-to-be ex-manager.

Pedro Martinez

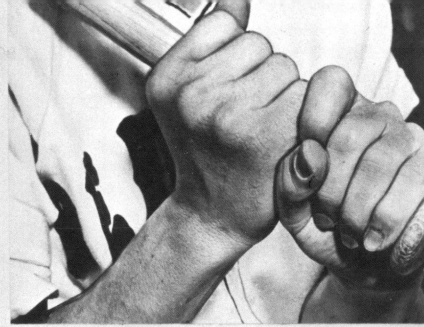

THE LITTLE PROFESSOR

In his later years, Ted Williams made a big push to get his old friend and outfield mate Dom DiMaggio selected for the Hall of Fame by the Veterans Committee. He didn't succeed, but a good case can be made for Ted's argument.

The youngest of three DiMaggio brothers to reach the majors, the soft-spoken, bespectacled "Little Professor" looked like he belonged in a chemistry lab but played like a Big Man on Campus. At 5'9" he could not generate his sibling Joe's power—few players could—but with a .298 lifetime average and four seasons over .300, Dom was still one of the American League's best hitters. He reached ten homers only twice but proved an excellent leadoff man by routinely placing among AL leaders in doubles and stolen bases, averaging more than 60 RBI, and scoring 100 or more runs six times—topping the league twice and averaging 124 from 1948 to '51.

Defensively, Dom was considered (along with brothers Joe and Vince) one of the top center fielders in baseball, and he set records for putouts and chances in 1948 that stood for 30 years. His Hall of Fame chances are hurt by the fact that he lost three prime seasons to World War II service and was later a victim of manager Lou Boudreau's overenthusiastic youth movement (DiMaggio quit at a still-productive 36 rather than become a backup), but the seven-time All-Star's legacy in Boston is assured.

Stellar Stat: DiMaggio's career mark of 2.98 chances per game in center field remains an AL record.

RED SOX/MAJOR LEAGUE TOTALS (1940-42, '46-53)											
BA	G	AB	R	H	2B	3B	HR	RBI	SB	OBP	SLG
.298	1,399	5,640	1,046	1,680	308	57	87	618	100	.383	.419

"*If we lose today, it will be over my dead body. They'll have to leave me face down on the mound.*"

—LUIS TIANT, OCTOBER 1, 1978. TIANT PROCEEDED TO SHUT OUT THE BLUE JAYS, 5–0, ON A TWO-HITTER TO SET UP THE NEXT DAY'S ONE-GAME PLAYOFF WITH THE YANKEES. HE NEVER PITCHED FOR BOSTON AGAIN.

BEFORE THE BOSOX

Boston was the center of the baseball universe long before the modern Red Sox ever played a game. The original Red Stockings, born in Cincinnati, had come east to the city in 1871 and emerged as a powerhouse in the first two acknowledged professional leagues—the National Association and the National League. The team would later be known as the Bostons, the Nationals, and finally the Braves, and it remains in existence today as the Atlanta Braves.

With baseball taking hold as America's pastime, the city that professed to be "the Hub of the Universe" due to its intellectual and artistic accomplishments could also lay claim to the game's best team and most fervent fans. Suiting up stars such as shortstop Herman Long, third baseman Billy Nash, and outfielder Hugh Duffy, the Bostons won five pennants during the 1890s alone and packed their beautiful South End Grounds ballpark.

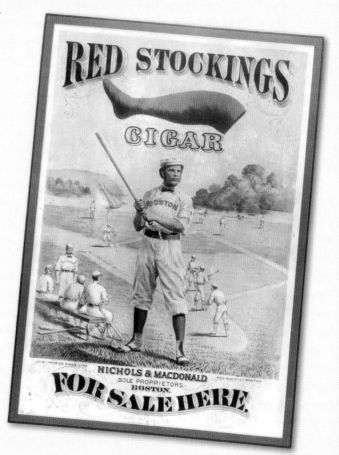

TED IS STAR OF STARS

He had already enjoyed two terrific seasons to start his career, but on July 8, 1941, Ted Williams blasted himself into baseball's highest echelon of superstars with a single swing.

Facing Claude Passeau in the All-Star Game with two outs in the bottom of the ninth, the 22-year-old Red Sox outfielder crushed a three-run homer high off the upper-deck facade of Detroit's Briggs Stadium to give the American League a 7–5 victory. Clapping and skipping as he rounded the bases, Williams was mobbed at home plate by his AL teammates. He later called it "the biggest hit of my life." At the middle of this season, Williams was batting .405; by year's end, he had raised that average one magical point.

THE TOOLS OF BRILLIANCE

It's been said that 1930s Red Sox backup catcher Moe Berg could speak in as many as a dozen languages but hit in none of them. Still, the .243 lifetime batter and Columbia Law School grad lasted 15 years in the majors with the Red Sox and four other clubs due to a keen wit and an ability to get along with people from all backgrounds. He was the consummate bullpen coach before the position officially existed, and after his playing days, he put his linguistics and adaptable nature to great use in another vocation: as a spy during World War II.

"BABE" RUTH
P.—Boston Red Sox
147

RUTH IS SOLD!

It was the biggest deal in baseball history—before or since. And in hindsight, it was clearly the biggest blunder as well.

The sale of Babe Ruth to the New York Yankees for $100,000 in cash and loans by Red Sox owner Harry Frazee, made official in early January 1920, linked the game's greatest player and biggest city just as both were entering their peaks. Ruth would become a worldwide celebrity while starting the Yankees on a four-decade reign of dominance, and his 54 home runs in the '20 season—more than those hit by any other American League *team* that year—signaled the start of the "lively ball" era.

A closer look, however, reveals why such a deal appealed to Frazee. Although Ruth had helped the Red Sox to three World Series titles with his pitching and hitting, the 1919 club finished sixth at 66–71 despite his then-record 29 homers. Now strictly an outfielder, at his own insistence, he was not a huge draw on a losing team, and his off-field proclivities for booze, women, and late nights upset clubhouse chemistry and irked manager Ed Barrow. If this wasn't enough, Babe was demanding that Frazee tear up his contract and give him a 100-percent raise to $20,000 per year.

The owner refused. "A team of players working harmoniously together is always to be preferred to that possessing one star who hugs the limelight to himself," Frazee said in a statement released after the Ruth sale was made public. "And that's what I'm after." Whatever Harry found, it amounted to a last-place club by 1922—when Babe's Yankees claimed their second straight pennant.

RED-HOT ROOKIES

Nomar Garciaparra, 1997

When Roger Clemens hurled his second 20-strikeout game in September 1996, he had only a few weeks remaining in his Red Sox career. The skinny guy playing shortstop behind him that night in Detroit, however, would quickly become Boston's newest legendary talent.

Nomar Garciaparra hit just .241 that month, but his official rookie year of 1997 was another story. Batting primarily leadoff, he set one record with seven home runs to start games and broke another with 98 RBI when atop the order. Pacing the American League in hits and triples, he had a 30-game hitting streak to set another first-year standard and earned the nickname "Spider-man" with his acrobatic plays at short. Clemens wasn't easily forgotten, but the AL's unanimous Rookie of the Year made his loss easier to take.

ROOKIE YEAR TOTALS

BA	G	AB	R	H	2B	3B	HR	RBI	SB	OBP	SLG
.306	153	684	122	209	44	11	30	98	22	.342	.534

The .300 Club

In 1950 the Red Sox became the last major-league team to maintain a .300 average for a full season—finishing at .302. Thin pitching relegated them to third place, four games behind the Yankees, but this lineup gave opposing hurlers nightmares all summer:

1B	Walt Dropo	.322	CF	Dom DiMaggio	.328
2B	Bobby Doerr	.294	LF	Ted Williams	.317
SS	Vern Stephens	.295	C	Birdie Tebbetts	.310
3B	Johnny Pesky	.312	UT	Billy Goodman	.354*
RF	Al Zarilla	.325			

*Goodman won the AL batting title despite having no set position. Who was he going to knock out of the lineup?

ROCKET UP, THEN OUT

After all the bad blood stemming from his angry free-agent departure, two world championships won with the hated Yankees, and the Congressional proceedings regarding his possible steroid use, it's easy to forget that Roger Clemens was once the most popular athlete in New England—and possibly the best Red Sox pitcher of the last half century.

From his breakthrough campaign of 1986 through 1992, the big right-hander was good for close to 20 wins, 250 innings, and 200 or more strikeouts a year, routinely leading the American League in ERA and shutouts. When Celtics great Larry Bird was slowed by age and injuries, the Rocket became the region's most electric athletic performer.

A Texas native who grew up worshipping the Lone Star State's original K King—Nolan Ryan—Clemens shot up through Boston's minor-league system and as a rookie recorded a 15-whiff game just after his 22nd birthday. Injuries held him back in his first two seasons, but on April 29, 1986, he trumpeted his arrival as ace with a record 20-strikeout, 0-walk performance against Seattle. Fans took to placing K cards up along the far wall of the Fenway Park bleachers for every Clemens punch-out, and by year's end he had 238 along with a 24–4 record and 2.48 ERA. He was in line to win the '86 World Series clincher and end Boston's 68-year title drought, but after the Series slipped away, he had to settle for being the team's first-ever dual Cy Young/MVP winner.

As recognition kept coming his way—including two more Cy Young plaques—Clemens became the face of the Red Sox. Aside from occasional hiccups, such as his profanity-filled ejection in the 1990 play-offs, Clemens delivered far more power than petulance. After Boston's drop from contention in the early 1990s, he continued making a mediocre team dangerous every time he stepped on the mound. He was also a hero with quiet visits to kids in hospitals and cancer wards.

Unfortunately, it all ended badly. In the lean years of '93 through '96 when Clemens went 40–39 and appeared to gain weight and lose speed overnight, his feuds with general manager Dan Duquette sometimes made more headlines than his pitching. He showed a flash of brilliance with a resurgent second half in 1996—capped in September by another 20-K game—but management's mind was made up. Clemens seemingly got the last laugh with four more Cy Young Awards and 162 more victories after leaving town.

KKKKlemens's Boston KKKKK KKKKount

YEAR	INNINGS	STRIKEOUTS
1984	133.1	126
1985	98.1	74
1986	254.0	238
1987	281.2	256
1988	264.0	291
1989	253.1	230
1990	228.1	209
1991	271.1	241
1992	246.2	208
1993	191.2	160
1994	170.2	168
1995	140.0	132
1996	242.2	257
Total	**2,776.0**	**2,590***

*Red Sox record

Only Two...

Only two New Englanders have hit a home run in their first major-league plate appearance while wearing a Red Sox uniform. Both did it at Fenway Park—Rhode Islander Lefty LeFebvre on June 10, 1938, against Monty Stratton of the White Sox, and Boston's own Eddie Pellagrini on April 22, 1946, off Washington's Sid Hudson. In neither case, however, was the feat a sign of power to come. Relief pitcher LeFebvre never homered in the bigs again, while shortstop Pellagrini managed just 20 in eight seasons.

IN THE DUGOUT: WALPOLE JOE

Reporters picking up the 1988 Red Sox media guide may not have noticed the photos of coaches Rac Slider and Joe Morgan reversed atop their modest bios, but there was no way to miss Morgan's picture in the '89 guide—it was alone on the cover.

Morgan went from afterthought to Miracle Man in the summer of '88. Hired as manager when John McNamara was fired at the All-Star break, the 58-year-old thrived as the club's first Massachusetts-bred pilot in nearly 60 years. The longtime minor-league player and skipper went 12–0 and 19–1 to start his big-league managerial career and captured AL East titles that summer and again in 1990.

Manager Moments: Fired after finishing second in 1991, Morgan left with a warning for management: "These guys aren't as good as everyone thinks they are." The Sox finished seventh the next year.

GROVE FINDS A NEW GROOVE

Though he didn't exactly come as advertised, Lefty Grove turned out to be a pretty good investment for new Red Sox owner Tom Yawkey.

After averaging nearly 25 victories over the previous seven years with the Athletics—and earning seven American League strikeout titles in nine seasons—Grove was acquired by Yawkey for $125,000 and two warm bodies in December 1933. When Lefty went a sore-armed 8–8 the next summer, A's owner Connie Mack reportedly offered to take him back. Yawkey said no thanks, and Grove rewarded his patience with six winning seasons. His good fastball was gone, but Lefty could still pitch—and kept doing so until eking out his 300th and final win at age 41.

Stellar Stat: Grove led the American League nine times in earned run average, the last four times while with the Red Sox.

RED SOX TOTALS (1934–41)									
W	L	ERA	G	CG	IP	H	ER	BB	SO
105	62	3.34	214	119	1,539.2	1,587	571	447	743

MAJOR LEAGUE TOTALS (1925–41)									
W	L	ERA	G	CG	IP	H	ER	BB	SO
300	141	3.06	616	298	3,940.2	3,849	1,339	1,187	2,266

TONY C IS HIT

When Angel righty Jack Hamilton's pitch crushed Tony Conigliaro's left cheekbone and severely damaged his eye on August 18, 1967, it was as if somebody had abruptly turned off the volume on *Sgt. Pepper's Lonely Hearts Club Band* midway through side one. The incident at Fenway Park was a jolt of reality interrupting a magical summer, and while the Sox and their shocked fans could quickly turn back to the pennant race for solace, the life of their handsome young star would never be the same. By the time Tony was 45, the victim of a debilitating stroke, that life would be over entirely.

How might the Sox have fared in the '67 World Series with Tony C? What might he have accomplished had his career not been cut short and two courageous comebacks not ultimately failed? Many think he could have hit 500 or more home runs (he'd already belted 104 at age 22). Instead, the kid who debuted five months after JFK's assassination lived out a life similar to Boston's most famous fallen hero—a dashing figure with an electrifying presence who shined bright, overcame great challenges, but eventually met a tragic end.

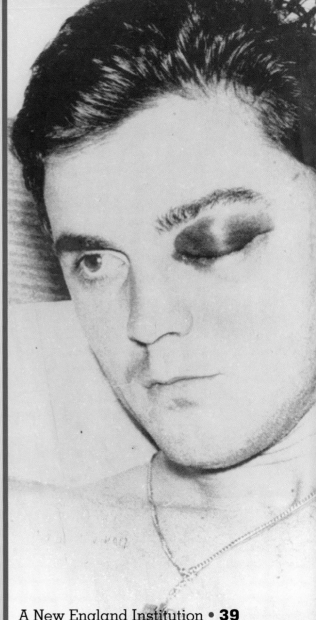

RED SOX/MAJOR LEAGUE TOTALS (1947–56)

W	L	ERA	G	CG	IP	H	ER	BB	SO
123	75	3.50	289	113	1,752.2	1,715	682	758	732

PARNELL PITCHES IN

Injuries cut his career short, but when healthy, Mel Parnell was one of the best left-handed pitchers to ever call Fenway Park home.

A New Orleans native who was a struggling spot-starter as a 1947 rookie, Parnell joined Boston's regular rotation the next year and went 15–8 with a fine 3.14 ERA. The lowball specialist emerged as the American League's top moundsman in 1949, leading the circuit with 25 wins against only 7 losses, 27 complete games, and 295⅓ innings. Although he failed to beat the Yankees in the crucial next-to-last game of '49, Parnell was seldom blamed for the club's near misses from 1948 to 1950 and enjoyed immense popularity with fans. The fact that he went 16–3 at home in 1949 didn't hurt; while Fenway's dimensions were usually deemed unkind to southpaw pitchers, Parnell was always effective there.

Parnell won 18 games in both 1950 and '51 and went 21–8 in 1953, when he shut out the dreaded Yanks four times. Then in 1954 came the incident that curtailed his career—a line drive off the bat of former teammate Mickey McDermott that broke the ulna bone in Parnell's wrist. He was just 3–7 that year, then won only nine more games before elbow surgery in 1956 prompted his retirement at age 34. At least the team's all-time winningest left-hander (for a season and a career) went out with a flourish—pitching a no-hitter vs. Chicago (at Fenway, naturally) during his final big-league summer.

Stellar Stat: In compiling a 123–75 lifetime record, Parnell went a phenomenal 71–30 at Fenway Park—a .703 home winning percentage.

"*A man has to have goals—*

for a day, for a lifetime—

and that was mine, to have people say,

'There goes Ted Williams,

the greatest hitter

who ever lived.' "

—TED WILLIAMS

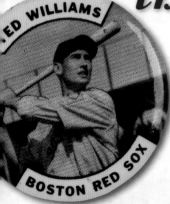

According to the experts, he got his wish…

"*Ted was the greatest hitter* **of our era.**"

—STAN MUSIAL

"*Whenever we'd* **play Boston,** *I'd get right up on the edge of the dugout steps when Williams was up,* **and I'd study him.** Ted Williams *is the best hitter I ever saw.*"

—MICKEY MANTLE

David Ortiz

FALL CLASSICS 2004 WORLD SERIES

Their history-making comeback against the Yankees in the '04 ALCS had meant so much to the Red Sox and their fans that many feared a letdown in the World Series against the St. Louis Cardinals. It took three batters in Game 1 to erase those concerns.

One out after the first two men reached base in the bottom of the first at Fenway, David Ortiz crushed a three-run homer. The Cardinals erased a five-run deficit in the middle innings, but Mark Bellhorn's two-run shot off the right-field foul pole in the eighth proved the game-winner. Curt Schilling (and his sutured ankle) bloodied up another sock over six stellar frames of Game 2, and key defensive plays by Series MVP Manny Ramirez (who also homered) and DH-turned-first-baseman Ortiz made Game 3 starter Pedro Martinez's last win in a Red Sox uniform his biggest.

Boston had gone the seven-game limit in their previous four World Series, so Sox fans were pinching themselves throughout the fourth contest. But when closer Keith Foulke grabbed Edgar Renteria's grounder and tossed it to first, generations of Red Sox Nation were wide awake to celebrate after 86 title-deprived years.

Classic Kernel: Game 4 victor Derek Lowe had also won the deciding games of the Division Series vs. Anaheim and the ALCS vs. New York.

Johnny Pesky

OPENING DAY, 2005—
RINGING IN A NEW ERA

It was a day their fans had long waited for—and their fans' parents and grandparents, too. On April 11, 2005, three generations of Red Sox players gathered at Fenway Park to celebrate the team's first World Series title in 86 years with 33,702 of their closest admirers.

The windy, 46-degree afternoon featured a little of everything to warm the hearts of those present. World Series rings for the '04 champs were carried across the field toward the Red Sox dugout by a contingent that included U.S. military personnel injured in Iraq and Afghanistan. Players, coaches, and other team employees were called out individually to receive their rings, with one of the loudest ovations going to the last uniformed recipient: octogenarian Johnny Pesky, then in his 64th year with the team in roles that had included player, coach, manager, and legend-in-residence. Making the ceremony all the more special was the sportsmanship displayed by the opponents who quietly stood and applauded from alongside their third-base dugout: the New York Yankees.

The "2004 World Champions" banner was raised up the center-field flagpole by Pesky and another icon of Red Sox yore—1967 Triple Crown–winner Carl Yastrzemski—as players past and present crowded around them and the Boston Pops and Boston Symphony Orchestra contributed world-class musical accompaniment. Then, after some of the region's most beloved non-baseball champions—Bill Russell of the Celtics, Bobby Orr of the Bruins, and Tedy Bruschi and Richard Seymour of the Patriots—threw out four simultaneous first pitches, the newest edition of Sox players took the field and whipped the Yanks, 8–1.

"It's just unbelievable," Pesky said after the festivities. "I never thought anything like this would ever happen to me." Fans who had endured many near misses getting to this point could certainly relate.

Chapter Two

PENNANT FEVER GRIPS HUB

"*I say the Red Sox ... sex ... and breathing.*"

—Fan Ben Wrightman
ranking the most important things in his life,
in the movie *Fever Pitch*

Capturing the pennant in 1967

RED-HOT ROOKIES
Fred Lynn and Jim Rice, 1975

Although the Red Sox squandered a seven-game AL East lead throughout the final six weeks of the 1974 season, Boston fans got their first look at two exciting young outfielders: Fred Lynn and Jim Rice. The next year, as "official" rookies, the pair helped ensure the Sox wouldn't fold again.

Lynn (*left*) was an electric performer on offense and defense. He took away home runs with over-the-fence catches in center and then blasted balls over the fence himself. Just after compiling a 20-game hitting streak in May and June, he had a Ruthian night on June 18 at Detroit: 5-for-6, 3 home runs, a triple, and 10 RBI. Rice (*right*) was less flash but plenty powerful, hitting tape-measure homers that reminded old-timers of Jimmie Foxx and Ted Williams. Initially a DH, he soon moved to left field and proved adequate defensively, with a strong arm.

By midseason Rice and Lynn were tabbed the "Gold Dust Twins." One twin's great year abruptly ended on September 21 after a Vern Ruhle pitch broke Rice's left hand, but Lynn and his teammates captured the AL East title the next week. The duo's final stats were nearly identical: a .331 average, 21 homers, and 105 RBI for Lynn; .309, 22, 102 for Rice. Lynn also led the league with 47 doubles, 103 runs scored, and a .566 slugging mark. This and his Gold Glove justified his topping Rice for Rookie of the Year and MVP honors (the first-ever dual winner). Rice was second and third, respectively, in the two votes.

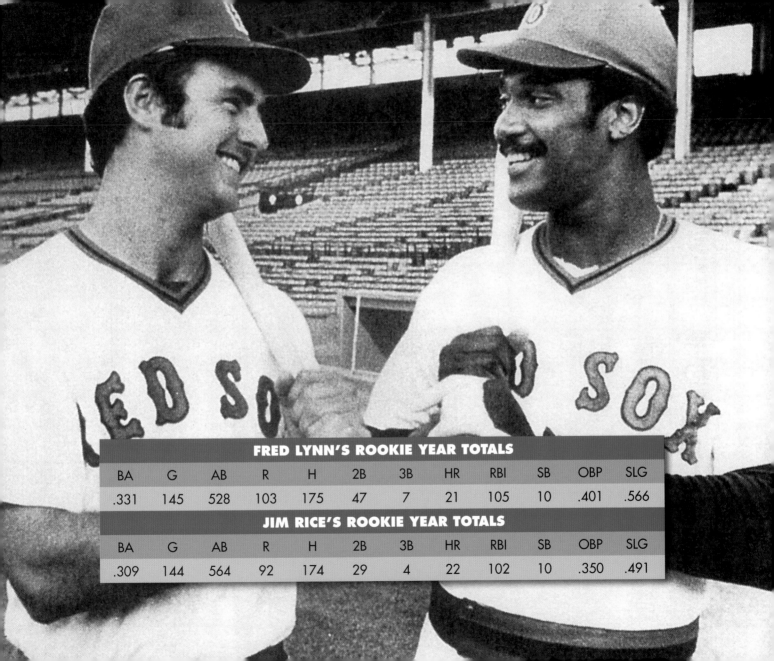

FRED LYNN'S ROOKIE YEAR TOTALS

BA	G	AB	R	H	2B	3B	HR	RBI	SB	OBP	SLG
.331	145	528	103	175	47	7	21	105	10	.401	.566

JIM RICE'S ROOKIE YEAR TOTALS

BA	G	AB	R	H	2B	3B	HR	RBI	SB	OBP	SLG
.309	144	564	92	174	29	4	22	102	10	.350	.491

PIERSALL PERSEVERES

He excelled as an outfielder, but Jimmy Piersall's biggest accomplishment was overcoming the mental illness that threatened to end his career.

Although his mother had lived much of her life being shuffled in and out of sanitariums, the Connecticut-bred Piersall seemed fine until he joined his beloved Red Sox full-time in 1952. There, under the intensity of the spotlight, Piersall's tightly wound psyche came undone. He fought with opponents and teammates, taunted umpires and fans, and started taking bows after catches. Eventually hospitalized in mid-summer, he discovered upon his release that he had no memory of his rookie season or breakdown. Piersall did, however, remember how to play. He went on to win a Gold Glove as Boston's center fielder and spent 17 years in the majors with five teams.

Stellar Stat: Piersall could hit too: He batted .293 with 87 RBI and a major-league-best 40 doubles for the 1956 Red Sox.

RED SOX TOTALS (1950, '52–58)											
BA	G	AB	R	H	2B	3B	HR	RBI	SB	OBP	SLG
.273	931	3369	502	919	158	32	66	366	58	.337	.397
MAJOR LEAGUE TOTALS (1950, '52–70)											
BA	G	AB	R	H	2B	3B	HR	RBI	SB	OBP	SLG
.272	1734	5890	811	1604	256	52	104	591	115	.332	.386

NIXON'S THE ONE

Oft-injured Trot Nixon never quite lived up to expectations in Boston, but the right fielder who was always getting his uniform dirty was a fan favorite for several years. He also proved to be a terrific clutch hitter, especially in the playoffs.

Case in point: October 4, 2003. The Red Sox trailed the A's two games to none in the best-of-five American League Division Series and faced elimination in Game 3 at Fenway. Boston took a 1–0 lead in the second, Oakland tied it in the sixth, and it remained knotted until the bottom of the 11th—when Nixon pinch-hit for Gabe Kapler with one man on and homered off Rich Harden for a 3–1, momentum-shifting victory. The crowd of 35,460 erupted as if the Sox had won the series. Two wins later, they did.

THEO AND THE TRIO, SHAPERS OF A NEW ERA

Whether playing baseball in the hallways outside his family's apartment or a few miles from Fenway Park at Brookline High, Theo Epstein had the same dream as countless New England schoolkids—to suit up for the Red Sox. Like most he didn't make it, but as the team's general manager, he did help shape them into World Series champions.

Epstein got his job in 2002 at age 28, making him the youngest general manager in big-league history, in large part because Red Sox ownership knew firsthand about his exceptional work ethic and evaluation skills. While at Yale, he had interned for the Orioles; after graduation, he moved on to the Padres—eventually becoming director of baseball operations. Larry Lucchino was president of both those clubs, and when a group led by Lucchino (as president and CEO), John Henry (principal owner), and Tom Werner (chairman) purchased the Red Sox in December 2001, one of the first things they did was hire Epstein as assistant GM. Within a year Epstein had the top slot, and "Theo and the Trio" were overhauling the Red Sox and Fenway Park in ways unforeseen during the staid 69-year regime of Tom and Jean Yawkey.

Within two years, huge stigmas attached to the franchise were disappearing. Long labeled a racist organization, the Sox had assembled a rainbow coalition of quality players from different racial and ethnic backgrounds. The new bosses modernized Fenway Park, deemed obsolete by previous owners, to preserve its charm while adding more seats and creature comforts for fans. Fenway tours, concerts, and additional luxury boxes brought in still more revenue, which was used to attract top-flight free agents and develop one of baseball's best farm systems. It all added up to unparalleled team popularity—and world championships in 2004 and 2007.

L-R: *Henry, Werner, and Lucchino*

OLD MAN YOUNG

More than a century after he threw his last pitch for the Red Sox in 1908, Denton True "Cy" Young remains a seminal figure in team and baseball history. The award for each year's top hurler in the American League and in the National League is named for him, and the big right-hander sits (tied with Roger Clemens) atop Boston's all-time leader boards for wins (192) and shutouts (38). In fact, Young's 511 total victories, recorded with the Sox and four other teams, may be the game's most untouchable career record in an era of five-man rotations and six-inning starters.

His nickname was the stuff of folklore: While Young was still in the minors, an imaginative sportswriter supposedly spotted him throwing warm-up pitches against a wooden fence. Noting that the ensuing damage rendered to the fence resembled what happened when a cyclone hit a wall, the writer shortened "cyclone" to "Cy" and pinned it on the hurler. The story might not be accurate—Young was also a farmer in the off-season, and his bench-jockeying brethren often dubbed such players "Cyrus"—but it added to his image.

Huge for his era at 6'2" and 210 pounds, he combined stamina, guile, and excellent control to stay among baseball's top pitchers for close to two decades. What makes his accomplishments all the more remarkable is how many of them came in his "advanced" years. Back in the early 20th century, long before personal trainers, pitch counts, high-tech exercise equipment, and arthroscopic surgery, the life span of a big-league pitcher was substantially shorter than it is today. Hurlers routinely burned out their arms and/or lost their effectiveness by age 30, but this strong farm boy seemed to get better after passing that milestone.

Young already had 286 victories when he jumped to Boston and the new American League in 1901, having entered the majors with the Cleveland Spiders in 1890. But after a 19–19 season with the Cardinals, he was thought at age 33 to be on the downslide of his career. He wasn't. From 1901 to 1904 he went 33–10, 32–11, 28–9, and 26–16, leading the league in victories three times and pitching Boston to two AL pennants and a World Series title. The starting pitcher in the franchise's first game ever, as well as in the first modern World Series contest, he helped bring immediate legitimacy to the new team and league, not to mention a huge fan base to the American League's heated competition with the incumbent National League.

Cy's accuracy never wavered, even as his waistline expanded. When the team slipped, he remained its top performer and drawing card. At 37, he pitched a perfect game, and he won 20 for the 15th and final time at age 41—notching an incredible 1.26 ERA and a second no-hitter in the process. That was his last year with Boston. Sold back to Cleveland, where his career had started 19 years before, he cranked out a 19-win campaign in 1909 before time finally caught up with him and sent him back to the farm after the 1911 season.

RED SOX TOTALS (1901–08)									
W	L	ERA	G	CG	IP	H	ER	BB	SO
192	112	2.00	327	275	2,728.1	2347	606	299	1,341
MAJOR LEAGUE TOTALS (1890–1911)									
W	L	ERA	G	CG	IP	H	ER	BB	SO
511	316	2.63	906	749	7,354.2	7,092	2,147	1,217	2,803

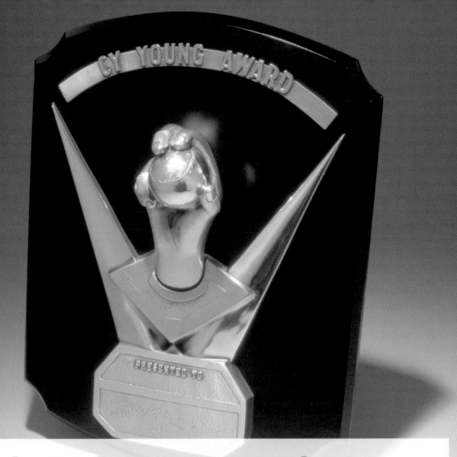

Red Sox Cy Young Award Winners

Jim Lonborg	1967	Roger Clemens	1991
Roger Clemens	1986	Pedro Martinez	1999
Roger Clemens	1987	Pedro Martinez	2000

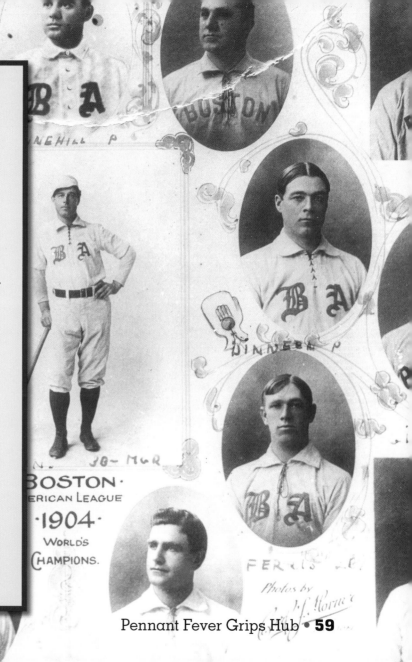

FROM AMERICANS TO RED SOX

From its first game in 1901 through the 1907 season, Boston's American League team was known simply as the "Americans." Although many team histories claim that more creative nicknames such as "Pilgrims" or "Puritans" were widely adopted during this period, they never really caught hold beyond a sportswriter or two.

The team's first—and likely last—true name change came about rather unexpectedly. During the 1907 season, Boston's National League club made a slight alteration to its uniforms by swapping the players' red stockings for blue. John I. Taylor, owner of the Americans, decided to adopt the red-sock look for his own club's home garb and took the name to boot. Starting in 1908, the Boston Red Sox would be taking the field.

BOSTON·
AMERICAN LEAGUE
·1904·
WORLD'S
CHAMPIONS.

FERRIS L.F.

Photos by
J.F. Horner

A RIVALRY IS BORN

They were not yet known as the Red Sox and Yankees, but in 1904 these rivals waged the first of many battles for American League supremacy. September featured 15 lead changes at the top, leaving the Boston Americans and the New York Highlanders tied heading into a five-game, season-ending series; whichever team won thrice would claim the pennant.

Boston took two of the first three and hoped to clinch at Manhattan's Hilltop Park on October 10. New York took a 2–0 lead off Americans ace Bill Dinneen, but luck was not with New York's 41-game-winner Jack Chesbro. A two-run throwing error by Highlander second baseman Jimmy Williams made it 2–2, and in the ninth a Chesbro spitball got past catcher Red Kleinow as Boston's Lou Criger raced in from third with what wound up as the winning run.

1904 Boston Americans

1904 New York Highlanders

MEMORABLE MANNY MOMENTS

It became popular during most of his stellar 2001–8 tenure to excuse the habits of a certain Red Sox slugger as "Manny being Manny." Seemingly indifferent play in left field, a penchant for admiring his shots from the batter's box, and off-beat comments to the media made Ramirez a lightening rod for old-school fans. Even his long, flowing dreadlocks came under attack.

Others, however, laughed off such foibles. If Manny sometimes loafed after uncatchable fly balls, he could also surprise with a great catch or throw. He liked to watch his shots, but so did the rest of us. Teammates appeared to embrace his playful attitude, and nobody did a better job protecting David Ortiz in the lineup or keeping Big Papi laughing. For 30 homers, 120 RBI, and clutch postseason performances, these apologists could handle a quirky Hall of Famer.

Then, midway through 2008, even they were swayed. Knowing the Sox would not likely offer him another long-term contract, Ramirez seemed to stop trying altogether. The laughs in the clubhouse stopped, as did many of the cheers. And even when Manny hit .396 with 53 RBI in 53 games after a trade-deadline swap to the Dodgers, fans embraced his ever-hustling successor, Jason Bay. Enough was enough.

Stellar Stat: Only two players in history—Jimmie Foxx and Alex Rodriguez—had more consecutive seasons of at least 30 homers and 100 RBI than the nine recorded by Ramirez from 1998 to 2006.

RED SOX TOTALS (2001–8)											
BA	G	AB	R	H	2B	3B	HR	RBI	SB	OBP	SLG
.312	1,083	3,953	743	1,232	256	7	274	868	7	.411	.588
MAJOR LEAGUE TOTALS (1993–2010)											
BA	G	AB	R	H	2B	3B	HR	RBI	SB	OBP	SLG
.313	2,297	8,227	1,544	2,573	547	20	555	1,830	38	.411	.586

THE 1975 WORLD SERIES

In future years, this would be the fall classic against which all others would be judged. Baseball's hold on the American public had been eclipsed by the NFL and bombastic broadcaster Howard Cosell in the early 1970s, but the Red Sox and Cincinnati Reds staged an epic battle that sent TV ratings through the roof and had the country buzzing about the original national pastime again.

It was a Series filled with characters and character. The ageless, ebullient Luis Tiant, twisting and turning his way to two victories—a masterful shutout and a 155-pitch epic—while running the bases like a determined bull. Boston's wonderful young athletes—Fred Lynn, Carlton Fisk, Dwight Evans—making clutch plays at the plate and in the field.

Cincinnati's dynastic lineup—Pete Rose, Joe Morgan, Johnny Bench, Tony Perez, George Foster—performing with grace and class. Bernie Carbo's *two* pinch-hit homers. The ever-quotable Bill Lee (*left*), who could also pitch a little. And, of course, Fisk's triumphal 12th-inning homer in Game 6. The finale notwithstanding, Carl Yastrzemski put it best: "I always thought that baseball was the real winner of the '75 World Series."

Classic Kernel: Yastrzemski and Rico Petrocelli, the only holdovers from Boston's 1967 World Series team, hit .310 and .308, respectively, to lead Red Sox regulars.

THE SOUNDS OF FENWAY

As unique as Fenway Park is to look at, it has also maintained its individuality for generations because of what fans *hear* while there.

From 1967 to 1993, what they heard first was the gravelly yet inviting tone of public-address announcer Sherm Feller starting each Red Sox home game with "Ladies and gentlemen, boys and girls...welcome to Fenway Park." The deep, distinctive drawl with which this popular Boston radio personality and songwriter introduced batters until his death in 1994 was imitated by fans throughout all of New England. Perhaps the ultimate compliment to Feller's legacy is that Fenway's current "voice" sounds as though he could be Sherm's audio twin.

When Feller wasn't at his mic in the old days, it was organist John Kiley's turn. The answer to a great trivia question—Who "played" for the Red Sox, Celtics, and Bruins? (he tickled the ivories for all three clubs)—Kiley *(right)* had a wonderful knack for finding the perfect tune for each moment. His most famous Fenway refrain in his 1953–89 stint was likely when he broke into the "Hallelujah Chorus" after Carlton Fisk's 12th-inning homer won Game 6 of the '75 World Series.

Kiley is gone now, too, and piped-in rock music has replaced the organ for much of each Fenway game. This no doubt displeases many traditionalists, but it has also led to new customs. To start the bottom of the eighth, no matter the score, fans join in a lusty refrain of Neil Diamond's "Sweet Caroline," and each Red Sox win is punctuated by the 1960s cult classic "Dirty Water"—which was written in honor of Boston's Charles River but has since become more synonymous with victory champagne than water.

EHMKE JUST MISSES DOUBLE NO-NO

There was little for Red Sox fans to cheer about during the 1920s, but right-hander Howard Ehmke did manage a near-historic pitching achievement late one dreadful season.

On September 7, 1923, Ehmke pitched a 4–0 no-hitter for the last-place Sox at Philadelphia. Facing the Yankees four days later, he gave up a grounder to leadoff man Whitey Witt that was fumbled by Boston third baseman Howard Shanks but ruled a hit rather than an error. After Ehmke retired the next 27 men for a 3–0 win, the enormity of scorer Fred Lieb's questionable decision became apparent. Ehmke had just missed throwing back-to-back no-hitters, a feat that has been accomplished just once in major-league history—by Cincinnati's Johnny Vander Meer in 1938.

NOBLE PATRONAGE

The city of Boston is known for its obsession with three things—sports, politics, and academics. A who's who of Red Sox fans shows that the three are often intertwined at Fenway.

Ever since Mayor John "Honey Fitz" Fitzgerald threw out the first pitch at Fenway's 1912 debut, elected officials have sought fun (and in some cases votes) there. Fitzgerald's grandson John F. Kennedy, a Massachusetts congressman and senator before he was president, was a fan, and U.S. Speaker of the House Tip O'Neill was an especially ardent rooter whose Fenway excursions spanned eight decades. As Red Sox success has soared in recent years, so have appearances by the likes of Boston mayor Tom Menino and Massachusetts senator John Kerry.

Among academic circles, there has been no shortage of Sox supporters. Yale President A. Bartlett Giamatti, before he became commissioner of baseball, was a Bobby Doerr devotee. Harvard professor/Pulitzer Prize–winner Doris Kearns Goodwin was reportedly the first female journalist in the home clubhouse, and Harvard biologist Stephen J. Gould wrote essays analyzing Ted Williams's batting. Then there is Purdue history professor Randy Roberts, whose book on Boston sports history was to go to the printer the day the Red Sox beat the Yankees in Game 4 of the 2004 AL Championship Series. The superstitious Roberts made the publisher promise not to send it until Boston lost—and seven games later the Sox completed their World Series sweep.

John "Honey Fitz" Fitzgerald, opening a pre-Fenway game at Huntington Grounds

Tris Speaker

Only Three...

Only three players have had hitting streaks of 30 or more games for the Red Sox. Dom DiMaggio's 34-gamer in 1949 tops the list, with other 30-game skeins recorded by Tris Speaker (1912) and rookie Nomar Garciaparra (1997). Johnny Damon (29 straight in 2005) and Wade Boggs (28 in 1985) have come the closest to joining this exclusive list, which might have even a higher number at the top had DiMaggio's line drive in the final at-bat of his streak not gone directly to Yankees center fielder *Joe* DiMaggio—who, Dom later recalled, "caught it in self-defense, or it would have hit him right between the eyes." Thanks a lot, bro!

MAVERICK ON THE MOUND

Free spirit, iconoclast, intellectual—these were just some of the labels put on Bill Lee. As long as the outspoken left-handed pitcher was winning, management endured his irreverence. But when his effectiveness ebbed, he was swiftly shown the door.

Lee began in Boston's bullpen but became a top-flight starter with 17–11, 17–15, and 17–9 records from 1973 to 1975. He tackled hitters with curves and sliders more often than speed and was particularly effective against the Yankees—a team he likened to the Nazis. But Spaceman offered his out-of-this-world opinions a bit too often for über-square Sox manager Don Zimmer, and when Lee slumped in '78, Zimmer buried the fan favorite on the bench in a move that may have cost Boston a pennant.

Stellar Stat: Despite being a workhorse with 51 complete games from 1973 to 1975, Lee struck out more than 100 batters just once—120 in '73.

RED SOX TOTALS (1969–78)

W	L	ERA	G	CG	IP	H	ER	BB	SO
94	68	3.64	321	64	1,503.1	1,627	608	448	578

MAJOR LEAGUE TOTALS (1969–82)

W	L	ERA	G	CG	IP	H	ER	BB	SO
119	90	3.62	416	72	1,944.1	2,122	783	531	713

THE SPACEMAN SPEAKS

Few Red Sox players were ever as outspoken as free-spirited pitcher **Bill Lee,** *or as fun. Here are just a few of the Spaceman's pointed comments through the years:*

"You have a left and a right. The left side controls the right half of your body, and the right side controls the left half. Therefore, left-handers are the only people in their right mind."

—ON THE HEMISPHERES OF THE BRAIN

"Tied."

—HIS ASSESSMENT OF THE 1975 WORLD SERIES AFTER GAME 2, AS DELIVERED TO NATIONAL MEDIA

"He counted the seams of the ball as it floated up to the plate, checked to see if Lee MacPhail's signature was on it, signed his own name to it, and then jumped all over it."

—ON TONY PEREZ'S TWO-RUN HOMER OFF HIM (ON A "LEEPHUS PITCH" CHANGE-UP) IN GAME 7 OF THE '75 SERIES

"That was no wind. That was Mr. Yawkey's breath."

—SPECULATION ON WHAT KEPT A HARD-HIT BALL BY REGGIE JACKSON FROM GOING OUT OF FENWAY DURING THE FIRST INNING OF THE 1978 RED SOX–YANKEE PLAYOFF GAME; JACKSON LATER HOMERED FOR NEW YORK'S LAST RUN IN A 5–4 WIN

"Zimmer didn't appreciate that, and I guess I should have apologized. To the gerbils."

—ON REFERRING TO SOX MANAGER DON ZIMMER AS "A GERBIL—A CUTE, PUFFY-CHEEKED CREATURE"; ZIMMER RESPONDED BY BURYING HIM DOWN THE STRETCH IN 1978

"There's nothing in the world like the fatalism of Red Sox fans, which has been bred into them for generations by that little green ballpark, and by the Wall, and by a team that keeps trying to win by hitting everything out of sight and just out-bombarding everyone else in the league.... All this makes the Boston fans a little crazy. I'm sorry for them."

—SPECULATING AFTER ANOTHER BOSTON LATE-SEASON COLLAPSE

SILENCING THE GHOSTS (PART I)

A fistful of mitt for A-Rod: That was the defining moment of the 2004 Red Sox season—a year in which the Sox finally pushed away ghosts real and imagined and stopped the chants of "Niiiiineteen-eeeeighteen!" that greeted them on each visit to New York.

It became popular over the years to call the long dry spell a curse, but nobody playing on the 2004 Red Sox believed that Babe Ruth or any-one else had kept them from a World Series title since 1918. The heartbreaking loss to the Yan-kees in Game 7 of the previous fall's American League Championship Series had left fans and players with a familiar sense of shell shock, but new manager Terry Francona instilled confidence and optimism that helped the Sox to a great start, including a three-game sweep of the Yanks at Yankee Stadium.

New York eventually overtook Boston for first place in the AL East and led by an imposing 9½ games when the two teams met at Fenway on July 24. That was when the Red Sox made a statement that would carry them through the rest of the season. Batting in the third inning, Yanks shortstop Alex Rodriguez—coveted by the Sox during the previous off-season—protested an inside pitch by Bronson Arroyo by yelling at the young pitcher. Boston catcher (and captain) Jason Varitek stepped in and used his glove to stop A-Rod's jawing, clearing the benches, electrifying the crowd of 34,501, and rallying his teammates. Trailing 9–4 in the sixth, Boston came back to win 11–10 on a Bill Mueller homer in the bottom of the ninth.

Infused by the incident, the team was fur-ther strengthened by a July 31 trade that sent disgruntled team icon Nomar Garciaparra to the Cubs and brought in defensive standouts Doug Mientkiewicz and Orlando Cabrera. The Sox finished second to the Yankees for the seventh

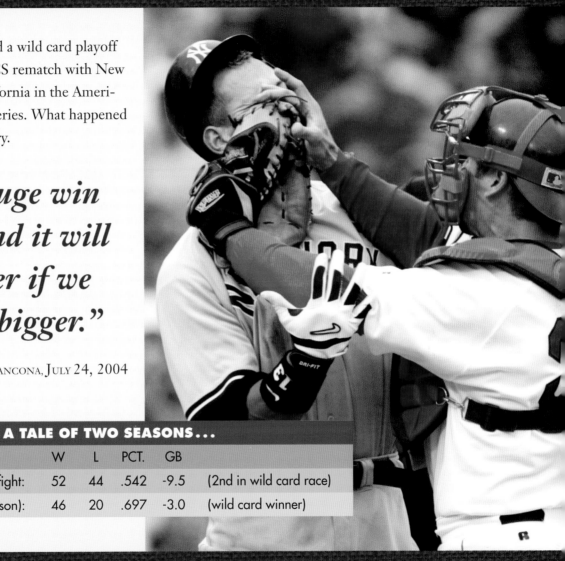

straight year but earned a wild card playoff berth and then an ALCS rematch with New York by sweeping California in the American League Division Series. What happened next would make history.

> ## "It's a huge win for us, and it will be bigger if we make it bigger."
>
> —TERRY FRANCONA, JULY 24, 2004

A TALE OF TWO SEASONS...

	W	L	PCT.	GB	
Before Varitek/A-Rod fight:	52	44	.542	-9.5	(2nd in wild card race)
After fight (regular season):	46	20	.697	-3.0	(wild card winner)

VOICES OF THE SOX
THE EARLY DAYS

Baseball and radio have been irrevocably connected since the medium came of age in the 1920s. The leisurely pace of the game lends itself to colorful description, storytelling, and memorable broadcasters, and through the years the Red Sox have had some of the best.

Excitable Fred Hoey was the biggest name in the early days, broadcasting both Red Sox and Boston Braves games over the Colonial and Yankee networks from 1927 through 1938. Back then only home games were covered live; for road contests, broadcasters staged "re-creations" in which they sat in a remote studio and described the action as they read it off incoming ticker tape that could be clearly heard "click-click-clicking" over the airwaves. But even though people knew Hoey wasn't actually *at* Yankee Stadium, they didn't mind—such was the power of the medium and its messenger.

Erudite Jim Britt succeeded Hoey during the 1940s on longtime flagship station WHDH-AM, and when television joined the picture in the late '40s, he called Sox and Braves games on both TV and radio. But Britt made one fatal professional mistake. When management from the two teams decided to go head-to-head on the airwaves in 1951, broadcasting home *and* away games, he was forced to pick one club to cover. He chose the Braves. After the National League club departed to Milwaukee in 1953, Jim was out of a job.

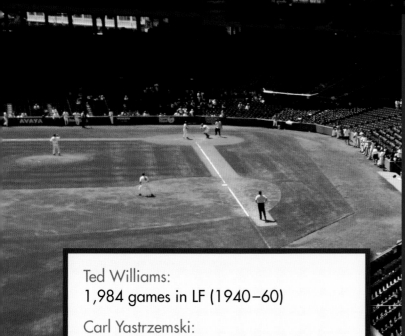

Ted Williams:
1,984 games in LF (1940–60)

Carl Yastrzemski:
1,913 games in LF (1961–80, '82–83)

Jim Rice:
1,503 games in LF (1974–88)

Mike Greenwell:
1,124 games in LF (1985–96)

Manny Ramirez:
837 games in LF (2001–8)

LEFT-FIELD LINEAGE

For the bulk of the seven decades since 1940, when Ted Williams moved to the spot in his second season, just five men have played left field regularly for the Red Sox: Williams, Carl Yastrzemski, Jim Rice, Mike Greenwell, and Manny Ramirez. Williams, Yaz, and Rice are already in the Hall of Fame, and Ramirez will likely join them. Greenwell doesn't have a chance at Cooperstown, but he was no slouch either—hitting .303 over 12 seasons with the Sox. Combined, the All-Star quintet won ten batting crowns and nine home run titles for Boston. Defensively, only Yaz was outstanding, but Williams and Rice both learned to play the tricky bounces off Fenway's Green Monster adeptly. Greenwell was justifiably maligned for his glovework, but while Ramirez also drew jeers in this area, he was capable of surprising fans with a nice running grab or leaping catch in the shadow of the Monster.

FENWAY IN FLAMES

Before it survived threats from the wrecking ball to become one of baseball's most beloved ballparks, Fenway nearly burned to the ground—twice.

On the night of May 8, 1926, a fire of unknown origin broke out in a pile of trash beneath the empty park's left-field bleachers, dooming the wooden-framed stands. Wind blew embers onto the grandstand roof, and soon the entire park was aflame. Firefighters managed to extinguish the three-alarm blaze and save most of Fenway, but cash-strapped Red Sox owner Bob Quinn used part of the $25,000 in insurance money to meet payroll rather than rebuild the charred bleachers.

After Tom Yawkey bought the Sox from Quinn in 1933, he spent his first off-season as owner overseeing a refurbishing of the entire ballpark. On January 5, 1934, while construction was well underway, another fire—possibly set on purpose, or maybe ignited by furnaces that workers used to heat the wood for the project—destroyed the center-field bleachers and spread to nearby buildings. Yawkey was undeterred, even by yet another smaller fire six weeks later. Employing three shifts of workers, he still had "New Fenway Park" ready by April 17, Opening Day.

STOPPING AT SECOND

In 1931, outfielder Earl Webb set a major-league record that still stands when he hit 67 doubles for the Red Sox. According to sportswriters, he used a tactic beyond just a strong left-handed batting stroke to reach this lofty total: He would often hold up at second base on shots to the gap even when he had a clear path to third. Of course, a few extra bases wouldn't have helped the team much anyway; the 62–90 Sox finished 45 games out of first. With attitudes like Webb's, it's no surprise.

TOM YAWKEY COMES TO THE RESCUE

After a 43–111 season in 1932 (the team's worst ever) and its 14th straight sub-.500 campaign, Red Sox owner Bob Quinn was nearly broke and seeking a way out. He found one in New York businessman Thomas Austin Yawkey.

Heir to a lumber and mining fortune being held in trust until he turned 30, Yawkey was the adopted son of a Detroit Tigers owner and had grown up around baseball. Itching to run his own team, he negotiated an agreement with Quinn early in 1933. Officially taking over less than three months after his momentous February 21 birthday, Yawkey installed his friend Eddie Collins—a former second base great with the Philadelphia A's who had attended the same prep school as Tom—as president and general manager. The two future Hall of Famers immediately began rebuilding the moribund club.

"I don't intend to mess with a loser," Yawkey told reporters, and he would not have to for long. The Sox finished 63–86 in '33, and the next year they made it to .500—a number they would remain above for most of the next 25 years. With Collins's guidance, the new owner began spending like no baseball boss had spent before, assembling a team of superstars that within three years included shortstop-manager Joe Cronin, outfield slugger Jimmie Foxx, catcher Rick Ferrell, and pitching ace Lefty Grove. All would eventually make the Hall of Fame, as would then-minor-leaguers Bobby Doerr and Ted Williams—both acquired by Collins on a 1937 scouting trip to California. Excellence and excitement had returned to Fenway Park, but championships would prove to be a harder task.

Tom Yawkey and his first wife, Elise

THE 1918 FALL CLASSIC

The horrors of World War I unfolded daily on the summer's front pages, but the Red Sox and ace left-hander Babe Ruth gave Bostonians a welcome diversion in 1918 while awaiting the news of their loved ones from the battlefields of Europe.

In a move conceived to free up ballplayers and make them eligible for enlistment or war-related jobs, the regular season was concluded a month early, on September 2. Ruth threw a shutout in the World Series opener, and in keeping the Cubs off the board for the first seven frames of Game 4, he completed a record 29⅔ consecutive scoreless innings pitched in Series play (dating to 1916).

The Sox ended things a few days later at Fenway Park—making them a perfect 4-for-4 in championship play during the teens—but this title was more subdued than previous ones. Crowds were uncharacteristically small due to the war and an ill-conceived boycott threat by both teams, who were disappointed that owners had cut their Series bonus money to let "runner-up" teams share in the bounty. Still, fans should have partied harder; Boston's next title would be a long time coming.

Classic Kernel: In addition to Ruth's 1–0 victory, Game 1 featured a band playing the first reported ballgame rendition of "The Star-Spangled Banner."

Chicago Cub Fred Merkle takes a lead off first with Carl Mays of the Boston Red Sox on the mound.

YOUUUUUUUUUUUUK!
A roster of Red Sox nicknames through the years

OLDIES (1901–60)

Catcher: Birdie (George Tebbetts)

First Base: Buck (John Freeman); Stuffy (John McInnis); Double X, Beast (Jimmie Foxx)

Second Base: Silent Captain of the Red Sox (Bobby Doerr); Pumpsie (Elijah Green)

Shortstop: Heinie (Charles Wagner)

Third Base: Rawhide (Jim Tabor)

Outfield: Spoke, Grey Eagle (Tris Speaker); Duffy (George Lewis); Baby Doll (William Jacobson); The Kid, Teddy Ballgame, Splendid Splinter (Ted Williams); Little Professor (Dom DiMaggio)

Starting Pitchers: Cy (Denton Young); Smoky Joe (Joe Wood); Babe (George Ruth); Lefty, Mose (Robert Grove); Broadway (Charlie Wagner); Tex (Cecil Hughson); Boo (Dave Ferriss)

Relievers: Lefty (Earl Johnson); Old Folks (Ellis Kinder)

Utilityman: One-Man Bench (Billy Goodman)

Managers: Rough (Bill Carrigan); Marse Joe (Joe McCarthy); Pinky (Mike Higgins)

NOT SO OLDIES (1961–2010)

Catcher: Pudge (Carlton Fisk); Geddy (Rich Gedman); Tek, Captain (Jason Varitek)

First Base: Boomer (George Scott); Hit Dog (Mo Vaughn); Youk, Greek God of Walks (Kevin Youkilis)

Second Base: Dude (Doug Griffin)

Shortstop: Little Louie (Luis Aparicio); Rooster (Rick Burleson)

Third Base: Butch (Clell Hobson); Chicken Man (Wade Boggs)

Outfield: Yaz, Captain Carl (Carl Yastrzemski); Tony C, Conig (Tony Conigliaro); Hawk (Ken Harrelson); Dewey (Dwight Evans); Jim Ed (Jim Rice); Gator (Mike Greenwell); Hendu (Dave Henderson); Pokey (Calvin Reese, Jr.); Coco (Covelli Crisp)

Designated Hitter: Cha-Cha (Orlando Cepeda); Big Papi (David Ortiz)

Starting Pitchers: Gentleman Jim, Lonnie (Jim Lonborg); El Tiante, Loo-ey (Luis Tiant); Spaceman (Bill Lee); Eck (Dennis Eckersley); Oil Can (Dennis Boyd); Rocket (Roger Clemens); Petey (Pedro Martinez); Schill (Curt Schilling); Dice-K (Daisuke Matsuzaka)

Relievers: Monster (Dick Radatz); Soup (Bill Campbell); Big Foot, Steamer (Bob Stanley); Oogie (Ugueth Urbina); El Guapo (Rich Garces)

Utilityman: Psycho (Steve Lyons)

Managers: Zim (Don Zimmer); Major (Ralph Houk); Walpole Joe (Joe Morgan); Tito (Terry Francona)

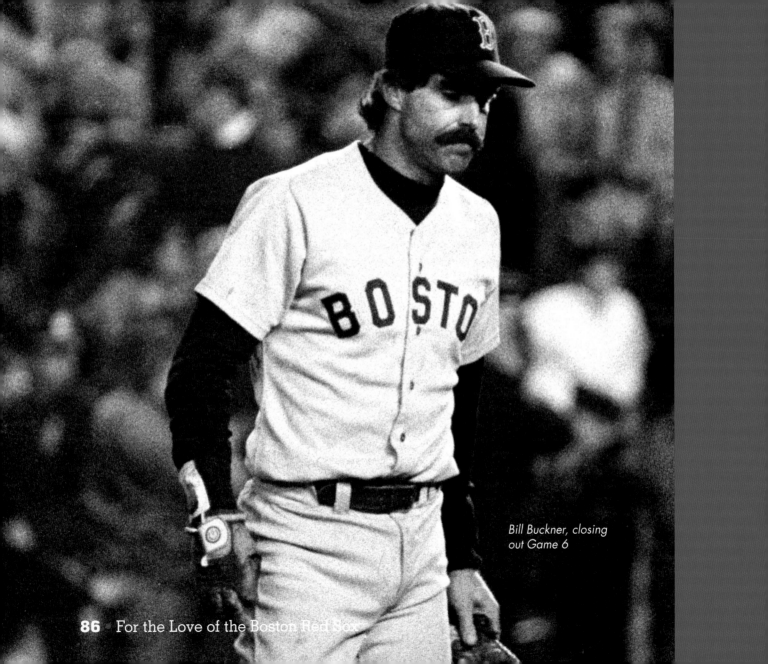

Bill Buckner, closing
out Game 6

NOT SO FAST WITH THAT CHAMPAGNE

Marty Barrett had already been named "Player of the Game" by NBC. Champagne had been brought into the Red Sox locker room, along with camera crews ready to record a victory celebration 68 years in waiting.

One sportswriter using a "wins matrix" formula later calculated that the odds were 1.4 in 100 that the Mets could take Game 6 of the 1986 World Series when Gary Carter came to bat with two outs, nobody on, and the Sox holding a 5–3 lead in the bottom of the 10th. But these were the pre-2004 Red Sox, and odds like that never worked in their favor; when Carter, Gary Mitchell, and Ray Knight all singled, stunned Boston fans knew what was going on. By the time Bob Stanley's pitch skipped past catcher Rich Gedman to plate Mitchell with the tying run and Mookie Wilson's grounder took a trip through Bill Buckner's legs to score Knight with the game-winner, it all made perfect sense. Once again, the Red Sox had mastered the art of losing.

RED-HOT ROOKIES

Johnny Pesky, 1942

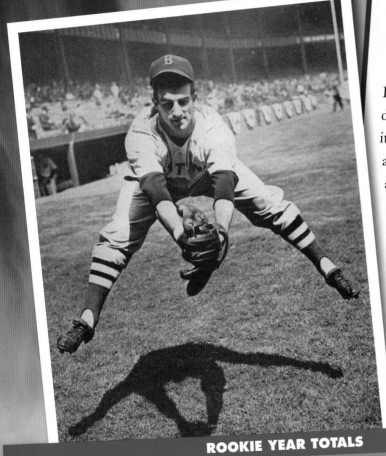

For those who have grown up watching Johnny Pesky dispense sage advice and endless fungos for the Red Sox, it may be hard to picture the Yoda-like octogenarian as anything but ancient. Back in '42, however, he was just another 22-year-old rookie hoping to stick in the big leagues.

He did so—and then some. After tripling and singling in his first game, Pesky stayed hot all season and finished second in batting in the American League to teammate Ted Williams while leading the circuit in hits. Sure-handed at short, he formed a great double-play duo with Bobby Doerr and placed third in league MVP voting. It was a season worth reflecting on, but Johnny didn't have time; immediately after it ended, he left for a three-year navy hitch.

ROOKIE YEAR TOTALS

BA	G	AB	R	H	2B	3B	HR	RBI	SB	OBP	SLG
.331	147	620	105	205	29	9	2	51	12	.375	.416

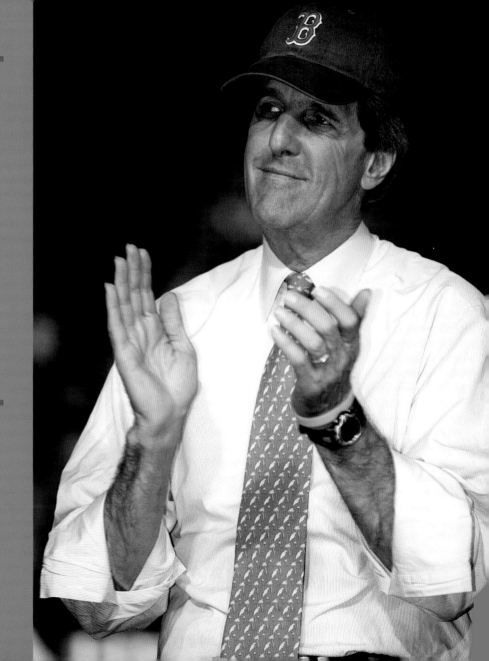

"*If anything prepares you to be president, it's being a Red Sox fan.***"**

—U.S. Senator John Kerry
of Massachusetts

THE MAN THEY CALL YAZ

He hit .266 as a fresh-faced rookie in 1961 and .266 as the retiring patriarch of the American League 22 years later. In between, Carl Yastrzemski appeared in more games than any other AL player—3,308—and all of them were with the Boston Red Sox. A generation of New England kids grew up, had their first kiss, got their drivers' licenses, and then left home while Yaz was suiting up for duty at Fenway Park.

The son of a Long Island potato farmer, a teen Yastrzemski played with his dad on semipro teams and spurned offers from the Yankees and other big-league clubs to sign with the Red Sox. Boston officials, concerned about his slight 5'11" build, were won over when he tore up minor league pitching for two seasons, and in 1961 he was trumpeted as heir to Ted Williams. Assigned uniform No. 8 (Ted's No. 9 had been retired), he took over the left field spot vacated by Teddy Ballgame the previous fall.

At first the pressure was too much, and Yaz's average hovered around .220 when Williams himself was called on to talk with the rookie. Apparently that session helped, because by year's end Yastrzemski was up to .266 with 11 homers and 80 RBI. He improved to .296 with 94 RBI his sophomore year, and in 1963 won his first of three batting titles and seven Gold Gloves. More fine years followed, but through 1966 Yaz had not yet fulfilled expectations; he had never hit more than 20 home runs, and the team was floundering amid eight straight losing seasons and dwindling attendance.

Then, after adding strenuous workout routines with a personal trainer to his offseason regime, Yastrzemski exploded in 1967. He won the AL Triple Crown (.326, 44, 121) and led a young Red Sox team that had finished ninth the previous season to an improbable pennant clinched on the season's final day. Whether it was a key hit, catch, throw, or baserunning play needed, Yaz delivered all summer. And while his .400 average couldn't get the Sox past the Cardinals in a seven-game World Series, he had sparked a Boston baseball resurgence.

The years to come brought many highs for Yastrzemski, and by 1975 he was the elder statesman on another team that fell just short in the World Series. More near-misses followed, but Yaz kept chugging along. In 1979 he became the first American Leaguer with 3,000 hits and 400 home runs—passing both milestones that summer—and by retirement at age 44 four years later he ranked first or second (to Williams) on most all-time Red Sox leader boards.

Stellar stat: Yaz also led the AL in slugging (.622) runs scored (112), hits (189), total bases (360), and on-base percentage (.418) during his magical '67 season. In the year's final two must-win games, he was 7-for-8 with six RBI.

RED SOX/MAJOR LEAGUE TOTALS (1961–83)											
BA	G	AB	R	H	2B	3B	HR	RBI	SB	OBP	SLG
.285	3,308	11,988	1,816	3,419	646	59	452	1,844	168	.379	.462

"SNODGRASS'S MUFF" OPENS THE DOOR

If Bill Buckner wanted to know what fate awaited him after 1986, he need only have studied the story of New York Giant Fred Snodgrass.

In the winner-take-all finale of the 1912 World Series at Fenway Park, the Giants led the Red Sox 2–1 when Boston's Hack Engle led off the bottom of the 10th with a high fly to center field. Snodgrass caught it two-handed, inexplicably dropped it, and then threw widely to second as Engle pulled in. Although Fred made a nice running catch on the next batter, and three teammates let Tris Speaker's foul pop-up drop between them later in the inning to set up a game-tying single, it was "Snodgrass's Muff" that lived in infamy when the Sox captured the game, 3–2, and the Series, as well. It even headlined Fred's obituary 62 years later.

Fred Snodgrass

Hack Engle

L-R: *Wes and Rick Ferrell*

RICK FERRELL'S RED SOX TOTALS (1933–37)

BA	G	AB	R	H	2B	3B	HR	RBI	SB	OBP	SLG
.302	522	1,791	221	541	111	17	16	240	7	.387	.410

WES FERRELL'S RED SOX TOTALS (1934–37) BATTING

W	L	ERA	G	CG	IP	H	ER	BB	SO	BA	HR
62	40	4.11	118	81	877.2	982	401	310	314	.308	17

THE BROTHERS FERRELL

As teenagers, the Ferrell boys of Durham, North Carolina, were always playing ball, with Wes pitching to Rick on various county teams. They kept up the practice as adults in the 1930s, but their playground changed to Fenway Park—and their opposition was the American League.

Quiet, even-keeled Rick and intense, tantrum-prone Wes formed perhaps the best brother battery in major-league history while on the Red Sox. Rick was an excellent-fielding receiver who hit as high as .312 and was a four-time All-Star with Boston. Although he belted just 16 Red Sox homers, he was good for 25 to 30 doubles a year, and he had a strong lifetime .378 on-base percentage. Durability was another plus, and his 1,806 games caught was an AL record for more than 40 years until broken by fellow Red Sox alum Carlton Fisk. Like Fisk, Rick is enshrined in Cooperstown.

Wes never made the Hall of Fame. He was 193–128 lifetime and, in his prime, was arguably a better player—and a better hitter—than his brother.

A 20-game winner his first four full years in the majors with Cleveland, the 6′2″ right-hander joined Boston a year after Rick in 1934 and went 14–5 for a mediocre club. In '35 he led the AL in wins (25–14), complete games (31), and innings pitched (322⅓); he also batted .347 with seven home runs—more than all but three teammates. Second in league MVP voting to Hank Greenberg, he followed it up with a 20–15 year in 1936 before arm trouble took away his good fastball. The next June, the brothers were traded together to the Senators.

Stellar Stat: Wes Ferrell's 38 career homers as a pitcher are a big-league record. In one 1933 game while playing for Cleveland, he allowed a homer to brother Rick of the Red Sox then homered himself later in the same inning.

CHAPTER THREE

THE WALL GIVETH, THE WALL TAKETH AWAY

"All literary men are Red Sox fans. To be a Yankee fan in literary society is to endanger your life."

—JOHN CHEEVER, AUTHOR

The Monster...before the seats

BIG PAPI, WALK-OFF WARRIOR

If they ever do yet another revision of the *New Dickson Baseball Dictionary*, a photo of David "Big Papi" Ortiz should run alongside the definition for *walk-off hit*.

Ortiz's reputation as Top Dog at ending games with one swing was sealed in 2004 when he garnered three extra-inning walk-offs in one 10-day postseason stretch—all at Fenway Park. He finished off Boston's sweep of the Angels in the AL Division Series with a tenth-inning homer on October 8, helped the Sox avert an AL Championship Series sweep by the Yankees with a 12th-inning blast on October 17, and then the very next night ended an epic 14-inning contest with New York by going "small ball" and blooping a single into center field to seal Boston's Game 5 win—and keep the team on its incomparable World Series–winning path.

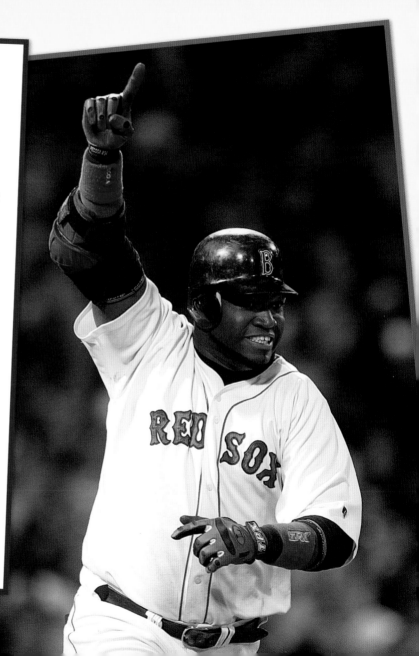

HARRY FRAZEE: VILLAIN OR VICTIM?

Harry Frazee with Red Sox manager Frank Chase, 1923

He may or may not have sold Babe Ruth to the Yankees to finance a Broadway play, but there is no denying that Harry Frazee made some bonehead moves as Red Sox owner from 1917 to '23.

For generations, Frazee's name was mud in Boston as team histories—many written by sports-writers who disliked the cocky, free-spending New Yorker—declared that the financially strapped theatrical producer had moved Ruth to fund his play *No, No, Nanette*. Historian Glenn Stout later asserted that Frazee was far from broke at the time and was instead the victim of a smear campaign led by AL President Ban Johnson. The aforementioned play, by the way, didn't even open until years later. Whatever the case, Frazee's moves that sent Ruth, Carl Mays, Waite Hoyt, Sad Sam Jones, Herb Pennock, Joe Dugan, and others to the Yankees mostly for cash shifted the American League's power base from Boston to the Bronx and became known as "The Rape of the Red Sox."

2,715 HITS, ONE RAW DEAL

Over the course of 22 big-league seasons, **BILL BUCKNER** batted .289 with 498 doubles and 1,208 runs batted in. When the Red Sox captured the 1986 American League pennant, he finished second on the team with 102 RBI and first in dirty uniforms. Fans who knew he had two injury-ravaged ankles admired Billy Buck's production—and grit.

Then fate decided that a certain ground ball—the one that turned the '86 World Series over to the Mets—go through his legs. Hounded mercilessly, his past good deeds forgotten, Buckner was first made a punch line and then sent packing. But now that a couple of World Series titles have dulled the pain of '86, perhaps his full body of work can receive the attention it deserves. And if he's made some money by autographing photos of the infamous play, can anybody really blame him? After all the ridicule, maybe that night owes Buckner something.

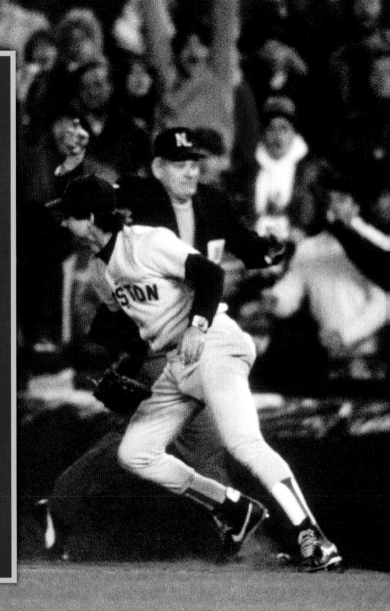

THE GREEN MONSTER—
UP CLOSE AND PERSONAL

The most unique characteristic of America's oldest major-league ballpark is without question its huge left-field wall. Fenway's "Green Monster" was not always green, however, nor was it always its current height. Here are a few facts about the spot where Red Sox sluggers from Speaker to Ortiz have taken aim:

Fenway's original left-field wall was a 25-foot-high wooden structure built to keep rooftop gawkers from seeing free ball games. Although some predicted it would take years before a ball cleared it, Boston's Hugh Bradley hit the first wall-topping homer on April 26, 1912—less than two weeks into Fenway's maiden season.

The wooden wall was replaced with a 37-foot version made of sheet metal and steel during new owner Tom Yawkey's winter of 1934 Fenway overhaul. Netting was added two years later to protect windows and cars on adjoining Lansdowne Street from slugger Jimmie Foxx's blasts.

Colorful ads blanketed The Wall in its early years, most notably pitches for Lifebuoy soap. When the company featured the tagline "The Red Sox use it!" smart-aleck fans quipped, "And they still stink!"

Yawkey had The Wall painted entirely green in 1947, leading to its famous nickname bestowed by an unknown source.

The scoreboard adorning The Wall is manually operated from a tiny, cavelike room inside it. Workers slid 12×16-inch metal panels into place each inning to update scores. Occasionally, they engage in friendly banter with Sox outfielders—Manny Ramirez was known to slip behind the 5′2″ door to say hi.

Fans looking closely at the scoreboard will notice Morse code running down one of the white lines adorning it. The dots spell out the initials of former owners Thomas A. Yawkey and Jean R. Yawkey.

After rookie center fielder Fred Lynn was knocked unconscious in pursuit of a fly ball during the 1975 World Series, padding was added to The Wall's lower portions in the off-season. A new fiberglass facing was also added. The original tin covering was cut up into pieces, mounted on wood, and sold for charity.

The Wall was once listed as 315 feet from home plate, but after the *Boston Globe*, using aerial photos and tape-measure readings, claimed it was closer, the Sox changed the marking to 310 feet. (Fenway's blueprints marked the distance as 308 feet.)

Giant Coke bottles first appeared alongside one of the light towers above the Green Monster in 1997, and the immensely popular "Monster Seats" debuted atop The Wall six years later.

Although the Monster Seats replaced the old netting on top, the ladder that workers used to climb up and retrieve home run balls, still adorns The Wall. A long fly ball that hits the ladder is considered "in play."

THE WILLIAMS SHIFT

If you can't beat him, switch things up. That was the logic behind the "Williams Shift"—a defensive alignment employed against lefty slugger Ted Williams in which the third baseman, the left fielder or shortstop, and the center fielder all moved from their normal spots over to the right of second base. This left just one man guarding the entire left side, but since Williams usually pulled the ball to right, it greatly increased the odds that someone would stop it.

Indians player-manager Lou Boudreau is almost universally acclaimed for devising the strategy in 1946, but while he used it *most*, it was actually White Sox skipper Jimmy Dykes who tried it *first* on July 23, 1941. Williams had entered the game batting a lusty .397 and still got a single and double against the stacked set at Fenway. It wasn't until July 14, 1946, that Boudreau first shifted, after The Kid torched Cleveland for three homers and eight RBI in one game. Other teams followed suit, but a stubborn Ted refused to give in by bunting or dumping the ball to left. Still, he got the last laugh with four more batting titles.

Bill Dinneen

Cy Young

Only Four . . .

Only four pitchers have won 20 games at least three times for the Red Sox: Cy Young, Bill Dinneen, Luis Tiant, and Roger Clemens. Young is the only hurler to do so on more than three occasions, reaching the magic mark six times (including two 30-win campaigns). He and Dinneen (who later took up umpiring) both earned their victories at the club's first home—the Huntington Avenue Grounds. After tiny Fenway Park opened in 1912, it took 65 seasons until Tiant made it a trifecta with his third 20-win effort in 1976. Clemens joined their ranks in 1990.

BABE BEFORE BROADWAY

He doesn't hold any franchise slugging marks because most of his days in Boston were spent as a left-handed pitcher, and he didn't do *that* long enough to amass gaudy lifetime totals. His last remaining Red Sox record—for 29⅔ consecutive scoreless innings pitched in World Series play—is all but forgotten, even though it was also a major-league standard for more than 40 years.

Make no mistake about it, however, George Herman Ruth was perhaps the biggest star to ever play for the Red Sox—or any other team. Nobody in baseball history captured the public's attention like the gregarious, headline-grabbing Bambino; no one else so excelled on the mound and at the plate. Other athletes had longer and more productive careers in Boston, but only Ted Williams can rival the dynamic hold the Babe had over the city.

His rough childhood spent in an institution for "incorrigible" youth—where Ruth learned baseball after being abandoned by his parents—explains the hunger with which he attacked life. Originally signed by his hometown Baltimore Orioles, a minor-league powerhouse, Ruth was sold to the Red Sox at age 19 and won his first big-league start the very day he arrived in Boston. More minor-league seasoning followed, but in his initial full season of 1915 he was 18–8 with a 2.44 ERA for the World Series champions.

Towering over most other ballplayers, the 6′2″ lefty was then a flat-chested athlete whose bulbous nose, large lips, and crude manners resulted in unabashed bench-jockeying and subsequent outbursts. Manager Bill Carrigan tried to rein in his free-spending, hard-living hurler, but while Ruth became known as Carrigan's "Babe," he was never controllable for long. His cocky attitude and feuds with management irked teammates, but he backed up his boasts with seasons of 23–12 and 24–13 in 1916 and '17. In the '16 campaign he also recorded a 2–1, 14-inning victory over Brooklyn in the World Series, helping Boston to another title.

The future Hall of Famer was arguably the best left-hander in baseball, but as it became apparent that he could also *hit* better than most position players, new manager Ed Barrow began using him in the outfield between his 1918 pitching appearances. He promptly batted .300, led the league in home runs, and still won the pennant-clincher and both his World Series starts against the Cubs (setting his record for consecutive scoreless Series innings in the process).

But after the Sox fell to sixth place in 1919 despite a record 29 home runs from Ruth, he and his huge contract demands were made the scapegoat. Owner Harry Frazee may have honestly believed selling his hot-headed, womanizing star to the Yankees would improve Boston's fortunes, but when the banished Babe ushered in the lively ball era with an astounding 54 homers in 1920, Frazee learned too late he was horribly mistaken.

RED SOX PITCHING TOTALS (1914–19)									
W	L	ERA	G	CG	IP	H	ER	BB	SO
89	46	2.19	158	105	1,190.1	934	290	425	483

RED SOX BATTING TOTALS (1914–19)									
BA	G	AB	R	H	2B	3B	HR	RBI	SB
.308	392	1,110	202	342	82	30	49	230	13

KKKKLEMENS
KS 20

On the night of April 29, 1986, most New England sports fans and reporters were focused on the goings-on at Boston Garden—where Larry Bird's Celtics were tipping off in a playoff game against the Atlanta Hawks. Those who instead ventured to Fenway Park, however, saw the emergence of another local sports legend as the Red Sox took on the Seattle Mariners.

Heating things up for just 13,414 chilly souls and a nearly empty press box, Red Sox right-hander Roger Clemens struck out five batters over the first two innings. Already 3–0 on the young season, hoping to fulfill the promise curtailed by injury the previous summer, the 23-year-old Texan allowed his first hit in the fourth but shortly thereafter struck out eight straight. A few fans started plastering hand-crafted red and white K cards to the wall atop the

bleachers—one for each of Roger's whiffs—but the Sox could not solve Seattle starter Mike Moore either, and the game remained scoreless through six innings. The Mariners went up 1–0 in the seventh on a home run by Gorman Thomas, but by then Clemens had 16 strikeouts and was nearing immortality: No pitcher had ever struck out 20 in a nine-inning game.

Dwight Evans gave his teammate the lead with a three-run homer later in the frame, and Roger responded with a perfect eighth while reaching 18 whiffs. The crowd was on its feet throughout the ninth, and Clemens didn't disappoint— fanning Spike Owen and Phil Bradley to reach a record 20 before Ken Phelps grounded out to end the game. All told, just ten Mariners had hit the ball in play; even more incredibly, The Rocket had not walked a single batter.

"Watching the Mariners try to hit Clemens was like watching a stack of waste paper diving into a shredder," wrote *Boston Globe* sportswriter Dan Shaughnessy. There would be plenty more slicing, too, as Clemens got off to a 14–0 start en route to a 24–4 season. K cards became more creative, as well. Those shown above featured the cast of *Cheers*, a TV sitcom set in Boston.

THE CLEMENS SCORECARD, APRIL 29, 1986								
First	Second	Third	Fourth	Fifth	Sixth	Seventh	Eighth	Ninth
KKK	7,KK	4–3,K,8	H,KKK	KKK	KK,8	KK,HR,1–3	K,H,K,8	KK,6–3

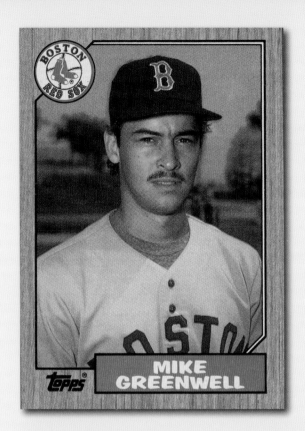

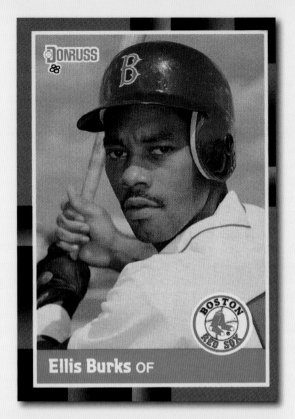

MIKE GREENWELL'S ROOKIE YEAR TOTALS											
BA	G	AB	R	H	2B	3B	HR	RBI	SB	OBP	SLG
.328	125	412	71	135	31	6	19	89	5	.386	.570
ELLIS BURKS'S ROOKIE YEAR TOTALS											
BA	G	AB	R	H	2B	3B	HR	RBI	SB	OBP	SLG
.272	133	558	94	152	30	2	20	59	27	.324	.441

RED-HOT ROOKIES
Mike Greenwell and Ellis Burks, 1987

One way to rebound from a disaster is to start anew. After their World Series meltdown in 1986, the Red Sox offered fans two fresh faces to help them forget: Mike Greenwell and Ellis Burks.

Settling in left field (Greenwell) and center (Burks), where veterans Jim Rice and Tony Armas had primarily roamed the previous summer, this Southern-bred duo provided a renewed spark to the Boston lineup. Greenwell was initially the better hitter—evidenced by his .570 slugging percentage and just 40 strikeouts that year—but defense often proved an adventure as he tried to solve the Green Monster's many angles. Nicknamed "Gator" because he supposedly wrestled the creatures back in Florida, the left-handed scrapper was a daredevil-type player whose hustle endeared him to fans.

Burks's average and slugging marks were a bit lower than Greenwell's, but the quiet, right-handed swinger from Mississippi was a graceful athlete who provided Gold Glove–caliber defense beside the Gator and a blend of power and speed rarely seen in Boston. Just the third Red Sox player (after Jackie Jensen and Carl Yastrzemski) to collect at least 20 home runs and stolen bases in the same year, he quickly moved into the leadoff spot and tallied 11 bunt hits. There would be no World Series redemption for the '87 Sox—or even a .500 record—but at least there was hope for the future.

DEWWWWWY

Two careers in one describes Dwight Evans. One of baseball's best defensive players, he had a laser for an arm and excelled in the challenging sun-splashed regions of Fenway's right field. At the plate, however, the eight-time Gold Glove winner spent nearly a decade as an inconsistent .260 hitter before suddenly becoming one of the game's top offensive performers.

The Red Sox thought the handsome, 6'2" California native would be an all-around star from the beginning, but in his 20s Evans was known primarily for stellar defense and sporadic power. He did excel in the 1975 World Series with a .292 average and several clutch hits, but it wasn't until the strike-shortened 1981 season that he began achieving his full potential. Reworking his batting stance under hitting coach Walt Hriniak, Evans hit .296, tied for the league lead with 22 homers, and finished third in MVP voting.

Manager Ralph Houk moved him from seventh in the batting order to the top two slots, and Evans became an on-base machine, piling up walks and runs scored while notching 20–30 home runs and 90–100 RBI a year. By the end of the '80s he had amassed the most homers (256) and total bases during the decade of any American League player. The Fenway faithful even screamed for "Dewwwwwwwy" when he returned to Fenway for his final season in an Orioles uniform.

Stellar Stat: Evans started the 1986 season with a home run on the very first pitch of the major-league campaign and finished it with a .300 average, two homers, and nine RBI in the World Series.

RED SOX TOTALS (1972-90)											
BA	G	AB	R	H	2B	3B	HR	RBI	SB	OBP	SLG
.272	2,505	8,726	1,435	2,373	474	72	379	1,346	76	.369	.473
MAJOR LEAGUE TOTALS (1972-91)											
BA	G	AB	R	H	2B	3B	HR	RBI	SB	OBP	SLG
.272	2,606	8,996	1,470	2,446	483	73	385	1,384	78	.370	.470

Only Five . . .

Displaying that rare (at least in Red Sox Nation) combination of power and speed, only five Boston players have notched 20 home runs and 20 stolen bases in the same season: Jackie Jensen (in 1955 and '59), Carl Yastrzemski (1970), John Valentin (1995), and rookies Ellis Burks (1987) and Nomar Garciaparra (1997). Dustin Pedroia nearly joined this exclusive club in 2008, falling three homers short.

John Valentin

TED GOES FOR BROKE

Walking the streets of Philadelphia the night of September 27, 1941, Ted Williams nervously pondered his fate. His batting average stood at .39955 with one meaningless day left in the season, and manager Joe Cronin had given Williams permission to sit out a double-header against the Athletics and finish with a mark rounded up to .400—a magical level not attained by a big-league hitter since 1930.

Ted was a perfectionist, and even at age 22 may have had a keen understanding of his place in history. Rather than take Cronin's offer, he decided to play. What happened next added to his growing legend: Williams went 6-for-8 in the twin bill (including a homer) to finish at .406. No hitter since has ever ended the season at .400 or above.

1946 WORLD SERIES

With the core of their lineup returning surprisingly sharp from World War II service, the '46 Red Sox rode a 41–9 start to a 104–50 record and their first American League championship in 28 years. Boston was a 3–1 favorite to win the World Series, but Sox bats would go flat at a most inopportune time.

Their Series opponents were the St. Louis Cardinals, who had captured the NL pennant in a three-game playoff with Brooklyn. The fall classic was a seesaw affair; Sox pitching was solid, but ever-reliable Bobby Doerr (.409) was the only Boston regular to hit over .261. Regular-season MVP Ted Williams checked in at just .200 with no extra-base hits, impacted, no doubt, by a bruised elbow he suffered in a pre-Series exhibition. Things still came down to Game 7, when

Harry Walker's double and Enos Slaughter's "mad dash" from first to home in the eighth gave the Cards a 4–3 victory and Bostonians their first-ever taste of postseason defeat. There would be plenty to follow.

Classic Kernel: Since-forgotten Tom McBride made the first and last out of the Series for Boston, but he also knocked in a key run during the team's Game 1 comeback.

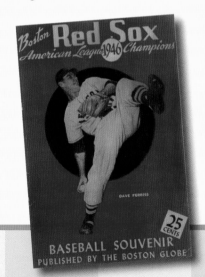

Enos Slaughter, safe after his "mad dash"

SMOKE GOT IN THEIR EYES

Injuries limited him to just two seasons with 200 or more innings pitched, but, when healthy, Joe Wood was one of the top hurlers in Red Sox history.

Up with the big club at age 18 in 1909, the right-hander was a 23-game winner within three years. His 1912 season was pure brilliance, as Smoky Joe led the Sox to the World Series title at 22. The next year, however, he hurt his ankle, broke his thumb, and—in trying to compensate for all that—may have impaired his shoulder. He never pitched pain-free again, and after piece-meal seasons of 11–5, 10–3, and 15–5, he moved on to the Cleveland Indians—and the outfield.

Stellar Stat: Wood's incredible 1912 season also included 35 complete games in 38 starts and a 16-game winning streak.

"WOOD" YOU BELIEVE?						
	W	L	ERA	SO	BB	SHO
Joe Wood, 1912	34	5	1.91	258	82	10

SOX STUMPERS: *The 1960s and '70s*

1. What rookie started at second base for Boston on Opening Day 1967?

2. He was the first African American pitcher to throw a no-hitter in the American League, and he hit a home run the same day to boot. Who was this fine 1960s right-hander?

3. This reserve outfielder cut down a scoring attempt by Chicago's Ken Berry for the last out of a key game during the 1967 Boston pennant drive. Name him.

4. Which highly popular 1960s slugger led the AL with 109 RBI in 1968 but was traded by the Sox the next April.

5. Who led the Red Sox with 19 victories in 1975 and got the win in Game 6 of the World Series?

6. Which future Hall of Famer, in his only season with the Red Sox, served as Boston's primary designated hitter in 1973, the first year of the DH?

7. Which two 1970s Red Sox teammates were also brothers-in-law?

8. This Vietnam veteran led the 1977 Red Sox in both saves and victories. Who was he?

Answers

1. Reggie Smith, who was subbing at second for injured fellow rookie Mike Andrews and shortly thereafter moved back to center field, where he played 144 games.

2. Earl Wilson, who was also Boston's first African American pitcher, debuting in 1959.

3. Jose Tartubull; catcher Elston Howard nabbed Berry with a sweeping tag at the plate.

4. Ken Harrelson, who also led the league in Nehru jackets while with the Sox.

5. Rick Wise, who also beat Oakland in the AL Championship Series.

6. Orlando Cepeda, who as a DH hit .289 with 20 homers and 86 RBI in his lone Boston season.

7. Rick Miller and Carlton Fisk; Miller married Fisk's sister, Janet.

8. Bill Campbell, who went 13–9 with 31 saves in 1977.

RED MARKS THE SPOT

It shines like a beacon in a sea of green, a spot officially known as Section 42, Row 37, Seat 21. The only red-backed seat in Fenway's vast outfield bleachers marks the spot where a 502-foot shot to right field by Ted Williams landed on June 9, 1946—or, more specifically, landed on the head of fan Joe Boucher. Williams's titanic homer off Detroit pitcher Fred Hutchinson—the longest ever recorded inside Fenway Park—was a smashing success, starting with the hole it punched in the bowler of Boucher's straw hat. As usual, Williams had good aim: Boucher was a New Yorker.

From the Beast to Big Papi

ALL-TIME HOME RUNS BY RED SOX BATTERS

1. Ted Williams 521
2. Carl Yastrzemski................452
3. Jim Rice 382
4. Dwight Evans.....................379
5. *David Ortiz.......................291
6. Manny Ramirez...................274
7. Mo Vaughn.........................230
8. Bobby Doerr 223
9. Jimmie Foxx 222
10. Rico Petrocelli..................210

*Through 2010

SINGLE-SEASON LEADERS

1. David Ortiz ....*54.....2006
2. Jimmie Foxx .... 50.....1938
3. David Ortiz .... 47.....2005
4. Jim Rice ....*46.....1978
5. Manny Ramirez........ 45.....2005
T6. Mo Vaughn.............. 44.....1996
T6. Carl Yastrzemski.... **44.....1967
T8. Manny Ramirez.......*43.....2004
T8. Tony Armas ....*43.....1984
T8. Ted Williams ....*43.....1949

*Led American League
**Tied for league lead

RED-HOT ROOKIES
Boo Ferriss, 1945

World War II cost the Red Sox the services of several star performers, including Ted Williams, Bobby Doerr, Dom DiMaggio, and Tex Hughson, but shining amid the hodgepodge of lackluster talent replacing them for the duration was one gem: pitcher David "Boo" Ferriss.

Discharged from the Army Air Corps early in '45 due to asthma, the 6'2" right-hander was promoted to Boston and promptly won his first eight starts (four by shutout). By late July, Ferriss was 17–3 and on pace for 30 victories; although allergy problems cooled him off, he still wound up second in the American League in wins, complete games, and shutouts for the seventh-place Sox. He even hit .267 with 19 RBI, more than Boston's first-string catcher Bob Garbark. Ted and Co. couldn't wait to see this guy up close.

ROOKIE YEAR TOTALS

W	L	ERA	G	CG	IP	H	R	ER	HR	BB	SO
21	10	2.96	35	26	264.2	263	101	87	6	85	94

SILENCING THE GHOSTS (PART II)

New Englanders knew the story, having been schooled in it from their first visit to Fenway Park. Ever since the Red Sox sold Babe Ruth to the Yankees in 1920, New York had won 26 World Series titles and the Sox, zero. In several seasons—1949, 1978, 2003—the Sox had been one game from doing in the New Yorkers only to see history repeat itself again and again... and again.

It looked like more of the same in 2004. The Yankees won the first two tight games of the '04 American League Championship Series at Yankee Stadium and then humiliated the Sox 19–8 at a chilly, funereal Fenway in Game 3. Boston fans hoped only to avert a sweep the next night, but the Sox maintained a steely resolve, caring nothing for the ghosts of the past or the fact that no big-league team had ever won a playoff series after trailing three games to none.

New York took a 3–2 lead into the ninth inning of Game 4, but with ace closer Mariano Rivera on the mound, the Sox showed heart just three outs from being swept. Kevin Millar walked, pinch-runner Dave Roberts stole second, and Bill Mueller singled him in to tie the score. When David Ortiz's 12th-inning homer ended the game, Sox players celebrated at home plate like they had won the Series even though they still trailed 3–1. Such confidence would serve them well.

New York led Game 5 at Fenway 4–2 going into the eighth, but once again Boston rallied to tie and then win in the 14th on an Ortiz single. Back at Yankee Stadium the next night, the Sox got seven innings from Curt Schilling in a 4–2 win during which blood oozed through the sock covering Schilling's surgically repaired ankle. It all came down to a seventh contest, as it had the year before, but this time the Sox wrote a different ending—riding six RBI on two home runs (one a grand slam) by Johnny Damon to a 10–3 victory, the AL pennant, and the record books.

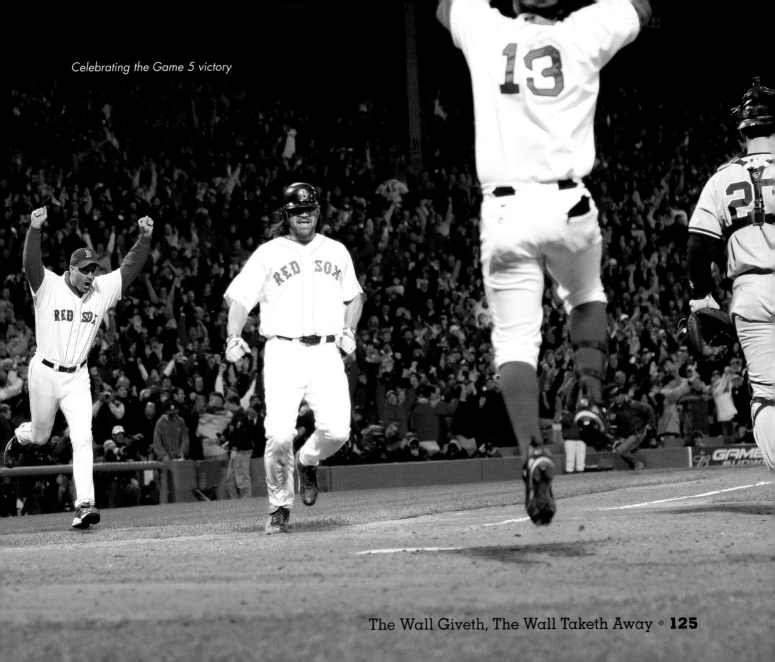

Celebrating the Game 5 victory

THROWBACK AT THIRD

To match some of his numbers, you needed to go back to Ted Williams; for others, you had to retreat all the way to Wee Willie Keeler. Five-time batting champion Wade Boggs amassed hit totals and batting averages at a rate unmatched in generations. Before most people knew what *on-base percentage* was, his was off the charts.

Incredibly, the biggest challenge the first-ballot Hall of Famer faced as a young third baseman was just making the Red Sox roster. Despite routinely hitting .300 or higher in the minors, this son of a military officer remained in baseball boot camp until nearly age 25 because he lacked home run power. (He hit just nine in his six minor-league seasons.) Boggs finally got the call to the majors in 1982, and when All-Star Carney Lansford sprained his ankle in late June, the rookie was handed a starting job at third. He responded with 26 hits in his first 60 at-bats, and by year's end he had an average of .349—an American League record for first-year players participating in 100 or more games (although he finished about 100 at-bats shy of qualifying for the league batting title).

Management traded ex-batting champ Lansford, and Boggs won his own title in 1983 with a .361 mark on the strength of 68 multihit games. Boggs's average was the highest in Boston since Williams's .388 in 1957, and it would stay above .350 for much of the next decade. Tailor-made for Fenway, he sent balls into the left-field corner or off the Green Monster with regularity and accumulated eye-popping totals as an unconventional leadoff man. He had 200 hits for seven straight seasons—nearly matching Keeler's record from 1894 to 1901.

Boggs, however, was not without critics. Some felt he could've helped the team more by letting his average dip in pursuit of additional home runs—he reached double figures just once for Boston. His defense also drew jeers early on, but he improved and became an excellent third baseman. He eventually won two Gold Glove awards, but only after Boston let him leave as a free agent following a .259 season at age 34. Boggs silenced those who said he was through by hitting .311 over the next four years for the Yankees, helping New York to the '96 World Series title and ultimately accumulating 3,010 career hits.

Stellar Stat: Boggs's .338 lifetime Red Sox average is the second highest in team history, behind Ted Williams's .344.

IT BOGGLES THE MIND						
Year	Hits	Runs	BB	2B	OBP	BA
1983	210	100	92	44	**.449**	**.361**
1984	203	109	89	31	.407	.325
1985	**240**	107	96	42	**.450**	**.368**
1986	207	107	**105**	47	**.453**	**.357**
1987	200	108	105	40	**.461**	**.363**
1988	214	**128**	**125**	**45**	**.476**	**.366**
1989	205	**113**	107	**51**	**.430**	.330

Bold = Led League

BROKEN BATS, BROKEN DREAMS

It's no longer considered the worst setback in franchise history (Grady Little and Aaron Boone took care of that in 2003), but the 1978 AL East playoff will always hurt because it denied a seemingly great team from even reaching the postseason.

The '78 Sox played nearly .700 baseball during the season's first half and led the East by nine games at the All-Star break. The Yankees, defending world champions, were 14 games out by mid-July but began rallying when combustible manager Billy Martin was replaced by Bob Lemon. Overly cautious Boston skipper Don Zimmer rode his starting nine without rest, and stale reserves forced into the lineup due to injuries failed to produce. Boston lost 11 of 14, and after New York swept a four-game series at Fenway by a combined score of 42–9—a weekend dubbed "The Boston Massacre"—the clubs were tied at the top on September 10.

The Yanks eventually stretched their lead to 3½ games a week later, but the Sox showed heart by winning 12 of their last 14 to catch them on the season's final day and necessitate a winner-take-all playoff at Fenway. Details of that October 2 game remain vivid today. Carl Yastrzemski homered off Yanks ace Ron Guidry for an early Boston lead, and Sox starter Mike Torrez held a 2–0 advantage when New York's light-hitting shortstop Bucky Dent stepped in with two on and two outs in the seventh. Dent fouled a pitch off his foot, and while he hobbled around in pain, Mickey Rivers noticed a chip in his bat and replaced it with one of his own. Torrez never warmed up during the long delay, and Dent sent his next offering just over the Green Monster in left for a 3–2 Yankees lead.

The advantage grew to 5–2 in the eighth, and though the Sox rallied to get within 5–4, the game ended with the tying run on third and Yaz popping up weakly against Goose Gossage. Boston wound up with 99 wins—its most since 1946—but with an even 100, the Yanks captured the division title and later the World Series. Few doubted the Sox could have done the same.

Dent's infamous homer

Carl Yastrzemski

"Let me get a good grip on the bat, as if I wanted to leave my finger prints on the wood; let me swing with a quick snap which comes from a powerful wrist, and, if I've gotten back of the ball it sure will travel."

—JIMMIE FOXX

"When Neil Armstrong first set foot on the moon, he and all the space scientists were puzzled by an unidentifiable white object. I knew immediately what it was. That was a home run ball hit off me in 1937 by Jimmie Foxx."

—LEFTY GOMEZ

TATERS AND SCOOPS

A powerful but streaky offensive player, large, lovable George Scott was without peer as a defensive first baseman.

Boomer was an All-Star starter as a rookie with 27 homers—the exuberant Mississippi farmer's son coined them *taters*—and hit .303 for the Impossible Dream team in '67. He won his first of eight Gold Gloves that season, and for years to come he scooped up everything in sight with a favorite mitt he dubbed "Black Beauty." After his hitting dropped off, a trade to Milwaukee sparked an offensive resurgence, and he tied the American League lead with 36 taters in 1975. Boomer returned triumphantly to Boston with 33 more in '77 before his gold-tooth smiles faded a year later.

Stellar Stat: Although Scott's batting average plummeted from .303 to .171 in 1968, he still played in 124 games and earned a Gold Glove.

RED SOX TOTALS (1966-71, '77-79)											
BA	G	AB	R	H	2B	3B	HR	RBI	SB	OBP	SLG
.257	1,192	4,234	527	1,088	158	38	154	562	27	.326	.421
MAJOR LEAGUE TOTALS (1966-79)											
BA	G	AB	R	H	2B	3B	HR	RBI	SB	OBP	SLG
.268	2,034	7,433	957	1,992	306	60	271	1,051	69	.333	.435

TED'S RUN CAPTURES THE FLAG

Just one of Ted Williams's 521 lifetime home runs was of the inside-the-park variety, but like most things he did, Ted made it a memorable one.

After posting a 96–40 record through early September, the 1946 Red Sox hit a snag on the cusp of clinching the franchise's first American League pennant in 28 years. Three cases of champagne remained sealed through a six-game losing streak and were back on ice when the Sox faced the Indians at Cleveland's League Park on September 13. Then Williams drilled a first-inning Red Embree pitch over left fielder Pat Seerey's head, galloped around the bases, and slid into home plate just ahead of the relay. Tex Hughson made the 1–0 lead hold up, and the Sox had their title—and their bubbly.

0-FOR-13

This was more than just Jose Canseco's batting line for Boston in the 1995 AL Division Series. Between Game 6 of the 1986 World Series vs. the Mets and Game 1 of the 1998 ALDS against the Indians, the Red Sox went 13 games through four different playoffs—*13*—without a single victory.

The streak started with Bill Buckner's nightmare in '86 and extended through a Mets win in Game 7, a pair of AL Championship Series sweeps by the powerful Oakland A's in 1988 and 1990, and a three-and-out drubbing by the Indians in the '95 ALDS *(pictured here)*. Boston broke the string with an 11–3 victory at Cleveland in Game 1 of the '98 Division Series, but then the Indians quickly took the next three games to win that round as well. By this point, Boston fans had to be wondering which was worse—never making the playoffs, or repeatedly getting embarrassed in them.

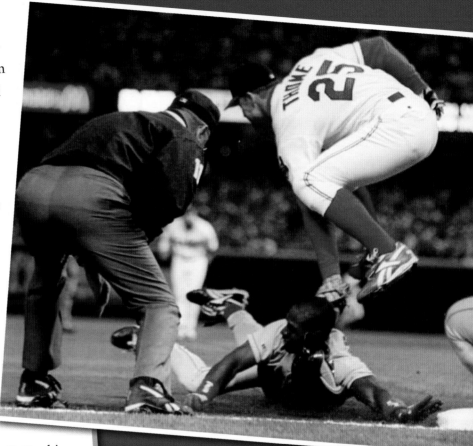

1915 WORLD SERIES

Although the Red Sox didn't win the pennant in 1914, Fenway Park still hosted the World Series that fall. The National League champion Boston Braves borrowed the venue from their AL neighbors due to Fenway's larger seating capacity—which translated into more postseason bonus money—and engineered a surprising fall classic sweep of the mighty Philadelphia A's. Then, after the Braves opened Braves Field—"the world's biggest ballpark"—in 1915, they returned the fiscally beneficial favor when the Sox captured American League titles that year and the next.

The 1915 Series was, ironically, another Boston-Philadelphia matchup, with the Red Sox battling the Phillies. The NL representatives took the opener behind 31-game-winner Grover Cleveland Alexander, but the Sox had such balanced pitching that they were able to leave standout starters Babe Ruth and Joe Wood on the bench and still win the next four straight. Boston hurlers held Philly to a .182 average, while Sox outfielder Duffy Lewis—usually known for his fielding—contributed a .444 average and five RBI for the champs.

Classic Kernel: Harry Hooper's two home runs in the Game 5 clincher (the second of which is shown at right) matched his total in 566 at-bats during the regular season.

PAPI ES SEÑOR CLUTCH

His smiling mug beams from the sides of buses and billboards, from T-shirts and posters and bobblehead dolls. David "Big Papi" Ortiz has become the 6'4", 230-pound face of the new Boston Red Sox, the key offensive force on two world championship teams and the consummate teammate whether he's doling out hugs and high-fives at the start of spring training or coming up with another big hit in October.

The man deemed by management as "the greatest clutch hitter in Red Sox history" came to the team in the humblest of ways. A platoon player for the Minnesota Twins early in his career, the hard-swinging Dominican showed good power but was considered too prone to injury and was released when the club couldn't generate trade interest. The Red Sox quietly picked him up as a free agent for the 2003 season, and he paid immediate dividends by moving into the starting lineup midseason and hitting 31 home runs. This was just a prelude for the '04 campaign, when Ortiz carried Boston to its first World Series title in 86 years, with 41 homers and 139 RBI in the regular season plus five more dingers and 19 ribbies in 14 postseason contests—three of which he ended personally with walk-off hits.

By the time he helped Boston to a second championship in 2007, Papi's name was all over the Red Sox and big-league record books. His 54 homers in 2006 set a new team standard—breaking Jimmie Foxx's old mark of 50 set in 1938—and he became one of just nine left-handed batters in ML history to register 30 homers and 100 RBI for five straight seasons (2003–7). Need a run? Page Papi: His 642 driven in over that span led all of baseball.

Stellar Stat: In his first five seasons with the Red Sox, Ortiz had 13 career walk-off hits—eight of them home runs.

RED SOX TOTALS (2003–10)

BA	G	AB	R	H	2B	3B	HR	RBI	SB	OBP	SLG
.286	1,141	4,213	760	1,205	308	12	291	932	6	.386	.572

MAJOR LEAGUE TOTALS (1997–2010)

BA	G	AB	R	H	2B	3B	HR	RBI	SB	OBP	SLG
.281	1,596	5,690	975	1,598	416	15	349	1,170	10	.376	.543

YAZ SAYS GOOD-BYE

Carl Yastrzemski scored 1,816 runs for the Red Sox, but it was a last jaunt outside the baselines that touched fans the most.

On the final weekend of the 1983 season, Yaz was feted at Fenway Park for his remarkable career of 3,308 games with the club— then the most in big-league history. The game on Saturday, October 1, included the official "Yaz Day" ceremonies, and although he went hitless, the 44-year-old honoree delighted the crowd by jogging once around the perimeter of the playing field waving and shaking hands. On Sunday, playing left field for the first time all year, he fielded a line drive cleanly off the Green Monster to hold Toby Harrah to a single and went 1-for-3 with a walk at the plate. Steady to the end.

"*The people kept saying 'We love you, Yaz.' I'll always remember that.*"

—Carl Yastrzemski, October 1, 1983

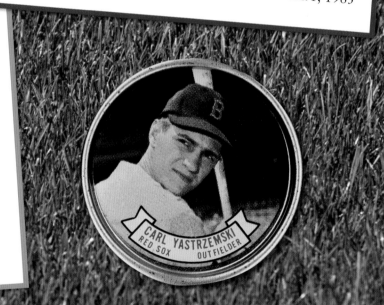

CARL YASTRZEMSKI
RED SOX   OUTFIELDER

The Wall Giveth, The Wall Taketh Away • **139**

IN TITO WE TRUST

Boston being Boston, there will always be those who jam the radio talk show airwaves and Internet chat rooms with questions about—or condemnations of—the moves by Red Sox managers. In the case of Terry Francona, however, it's hard to argue the facts: "Tito" is the most successful field boss in team history.

Two World Series titles, five playoff appearances, and an average of 93 regular-season wins over his first seven seasons (through 2010) is only part of the story. While a few standout players—David Ortiz, Jason Varitek, Tim Wakefield—were onboard throughout that run, Francona has shined by keeping *all* his athletes poised and ready to produce even if unhappy. When media and fans wanted to hand Coco Crisp's center-field job to rookie World Series hero Jacoby Ellsbury in early 2008, for instance, Francona praised both players and found a way to keep both in-

volved. Crisp sat more than he wanted, but he shined when given the chance in the postseason.

Francona's first Sox team, in 2004, had to overcome a far larger challenge—the trade of iconic shortstop Nomar Garciaparra to the Chicago Cubs in mid-season—but here, too, the manager rallied his troops. When Boston was down three games to none against the Yankees in the AL Championship Series that fall, or when they faced a three games to one deficit to Cleveland in the 2007 ALCS, Sox players maintained their confidence and rallied to win the pennant and sweep the World Series in both instances. Even when the team suffered a seemingly endless string of injuries in 2010, it stayed in the Wild Card race until the final week under Tito's stewardship.

A life lived within the game certainly helped shape Francona's approach. His father—the original Tito—was a big-league outfielder from 1956 to '70, and Terry grew up hanging around star-studded locker rooms. His own promising career in the majors petered out due in part to injuries, but as a manager he's earned the respect of his players by backing them, shunning the spotlight, laughing off talk-show critics, and maintaining his composure in a baseball-frenzied market where none of those tasks are easy.

"He cares what his players think, what his organization thinks, what his family thinks, and I don't think he really cares beyond that."

—Curt Schilling

CALL THE SEVENTH GAME OFF

"He swings—long drive, left field....
If it stays fair it's gonnnne....Home run!!"

—NED MARTIN,
SOX ANNOUNCER,
12:34 A.M., OCTOBER 21, 1975

Carlton Fisk

NEW PARK IN THE FENS

Boston's first opponent in its new ballpark was the New York Highlanders, soon to become the Yankees. First ball duties were handled by Boston Mayor John "Honey Fitz" Fitzgerald, John F. Kennedy's grandfather. Talk in the stands focused on the sinking of the RMS *Titanic* five days earlier. It was April 20, 1912, and some 27,000 baseball fans were assembled for the unveiling of what has since become perhaps baseball's most beloved venue: Fenway Park.

It was a new era for the Red Sox and the game. For the first 11 years of its existence, the team had played in the Huntington Avenue Grounds, a modest wooden ballpark within the city's South End neighborhood. But other big-league franchises had begun building more durable steel and concrete venues that were fireproof and offered far greater seating capacity. Sox owner John I. Taylor, who was more interested in real estate (and money) than baseball, was excited to join the trend.

He chose a spot in Boston's Fenway area, about a mile from the Huntington Avenue Grounds. "The Fens" once consisted of foul-smelling mud flats, but it had been converted into a pleasant, park-laden district by famed landscape architect Frederick Law Olmsted. Taylor purchased the land for $300,000 from his father's Fenway Realty Company, got his dad free publicity by conceiving the name Fenway Park, and started construction in the winter of 1911. Architect James McLaughlin's original plans for a second deck were scrapped so that the park could be ready for Opening Day, and when that day came, the Sox sent the fans home happy with a 7–6 victory in 11 innings.

STEAMER

A Maine native who appeared in more games than any other Red Sox pitcher, swingman Bob Stanley was on the mound for two of the worst moments in team history—but he had many more highs than lows in his versatile career.

After a solid rookie season, Steamer went 15–2 with ten saves in 1978, but his gopher pitch to Reggie Jackson resulted in the final margin of the Yankees' 5–4 playoff win. The right-hander rebounded with a 16–12 mark as a full-time starter in '79, then he switched back to the pen and had 33 saves a few years later. He couldn't quite close out the 1986 World Series, but, like Bill Buckner, he deserves a better fate—there was plenty of blame to go around.

Stellar Stat: Stanley's 637 games pitched are a whopping 133 ahead of Tim Wakefield, who is second in appearances for Boston (through 2008).

RED SOX/MAJOR LEAGUE TOTALS (1977-89)									
W	L	ERA	G	CG	IP	H	ER	BB	SO
115	97	3.64	637	21	1,707	1,858	690	471	693

BRUNO TO THE (HIDDEN) RESCUE

It was one of the most important catches in Red Sox history, but at first most people at Fenway Park couldn't tell if it had even been made.

The 1990 Red Sox led the Toronto Blue Jays by one game in the American League East and had a chance to clinch a division title with a win over the White Sox on the season's final day. Boston had a 3–1 advantage going into the ninth, but Chicago had the tying runs on first and second with two outs when Ozzie Guillen hit a liner toward the right-field corner. Tom Brunansky sprinted over, went into a slide, and then disappeared from most people's view. First base umpire Tim McClellan, fortunately, did see Bruno catch the ball just before it hit the ground—and Boston had its title.

CY IS SUPERB

Including postseason play, there had been 16,959 games in Red Sox history through 2008, but the team's only truly perfect day of pitching was turned in by the same man who had started the franchise's very first contest: Cy Young.

On May 5, 1904, 37-year-old Young took to the mound at Boston's Huntington Avenue Grounds to face Philadelphia A's ace Rube Waddell. Boston took a 3–0 lead in the late innings, and a buzz spread throughout the scoreboard-less ballpark that something special was happening. Waddell himself was the final man to face Young, and when he flew out, the crowd of around 10,000 erupted. In just 83 minutes, "The King of Pitchers" had faced 27 men and retired them all for baseball's first perfect game in 24 years.

NEAR MISSES (PART I)

The only thing more excruciating for Red Sox fans than waiting 86 years between World Series titles was how agonizingly close the club came to breaking the dry spell on numerous occasions. Boston's first wave of heartbreak came immediately following World War II. The 1946 team breezed to the American League pennant with a 104–50 mark but lost to St. Louis in a thrilling seven-game World Series decided on Enos Slaughter's "mad dash" home in the finale. The Sox had a down year in '47 due to pitching injuries, but in 1948 they battled with the Yankees and Indians all year before winding up tied for first with Cleveland at season's end. A one-game playoff was held at Fenway, and the Indians prevailed 8–3 when Sox manager Joe McCarthy gambled and lost on journeyman pitcher Denny Galehouse (just 8–7) as his surprise starter. McCarthy was back at the helm again in '49, and after another grueling regular season fight, he had his team poised to win the AL title at Yankee Stadium on the final weekend. Just one win in two games was needed this time, but the Sox lost them both, 5–4 and 5–3, giving New York the pennant.

L-R: Ted Williams, Jack Kramer, Birdie Tebbetts

COLLINS AT THE HOT CORNER

In addition to being a consensus pick as the greatest third baseman of baseball's early years, Jimmy Collins was one of the central figures in the battle for Boston diamond supremacy at the turn of the 20th century. His defection from the city's National League team to its new American League entry helped the AL establish itself as a viable second circuit, and as the first Red Sox manager he was idolized for leading the 1903 club to a championship in the inaugural "modern" World Series. Of course, being a tough, good-looking Irish lad didn't hurt his popularity in Boston, either.

A slight, 5'7", 160-pound outfielder in his youth who didn't make the big leagues until 1895 at age 25, the Buffalo-born Collins struggled as a rookie for the powerful Boston Nationals and was "loaned" to a weaker NL franchise in Louisville. By the time he came back to Boston in '96, he was a converted third baseman, perfecting such then-innovative techniques as playing off or behind the bag and running in full-tilt to scoop up bunts bare-handed and throw to first in one continuous motion. In 1899 he had 601 accepted chances, still an NL record, and his tactics forced teams that once used the bunt almost exclusively to expand their offensive repertoire.

After helping the Nationals to pennants in 1897 and '98 with averages of .346 and .328, Collins was at the peak of his fame. This made him a logical target for offers from owner Charles Somers to join Boston's new AL franchise. He took the bait of a big salary boost to "jump" to the American League in 1901, and many Boston fans did the same by moving their allegiances literally across the railroad tracks from the National League's South End Grounds ballpark to the AL's brand-new Huntington Avenue Grounds. "I like to play baseball," their hero said, "but this is a business with me. . . . I look out for James J. Collins."

Installed as player-manager, Collins hit .332 that first AL summer and remained a strong contributor for years. He managed the club to five straight winning seasons, including pennants in '03 and '04 and the '03 world championship. He still ranks high on the club's all-time lists in fielding percentage, putouts, and assists. Given his role at developing the position, his choice in 1945 as the first full-time third baseman named to the Hall of Fame was an appropriate one.

Stellar Stat: Collins hit just 25 dead-ball homers in seven Red Sox seasons, but from 1901 to '04 he averaged 32 doubles and 14 triples per year.

RED SOX TOTALS (1901-07)											
BA	G	AB	R	H	2B	3B	HR	RBI	SB	OBP	SLG
.296	741	2,972	448	881	171	65	25	385	102	.328	.423
MAJOR LEAGUE TOTALS (1895-1908)											
BA	G	AB	R	H	2B	3B	HR	RBI	SB	OBP	SLG
.294	1,725	6,795	1,055	1,999	352	116	65	983	194	.343	.409

"As soon as I got out there I felt a strange relationship with the pitcher's mound. It was as if I'd been born out there. Pitching just felt like the most natural thing in the world. Striking out batters was easy."

—BABE RUTH,
THE AMERICAN LEAGUE'S BEST LEFT-HANDED HURLER
WHILE WITH THE RED SOX

"Born? Hell, Babe Ruth wasn't born. He fell from a tree."

—JOE DUGAN,
RUTH'S TEAMMATE ON THE RED SOX AND YANKEES

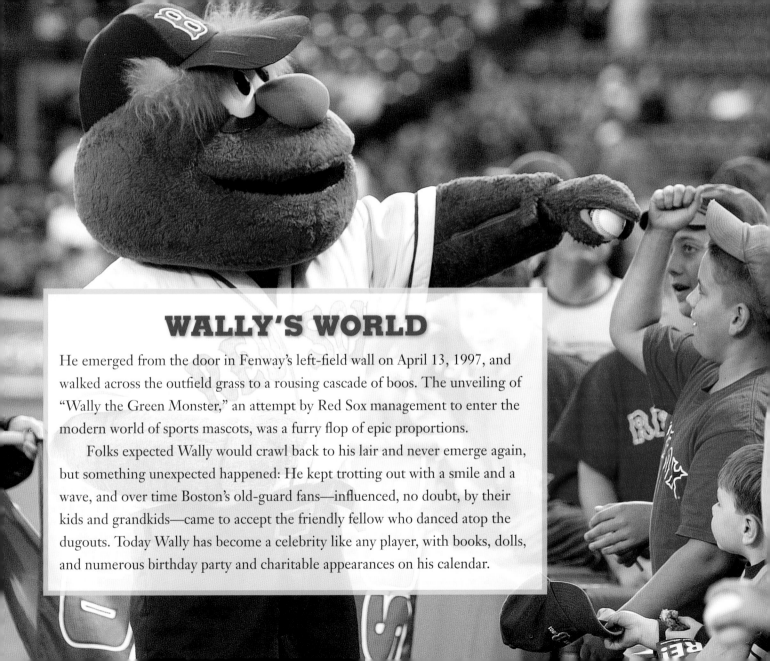

WALLY'S WORLD

He emerged from the door in Fenway's left-field wall on April 13, 1997, and walked across the outfield grass to a rousing cascade of boos. The unveiling of "Wally the Green Monster," an attempt by Red Sox management to enter the modern world of sports mascots, was a furry flop of epic proportions.

Folks expected Wally would crawl back to his lair and never emerge again, but something unexpected happened: He kept trotting out with a smile and a wave, and over time Boston's old-guard fans—influenced, no doubt, by their kids and grandkids—came to accept the friendly fellow who danced atop the dugouts. Today Wally has become a celebrity like any player, with books, dolls, and numerous birthday party and charitable appearances on his calendar.

Ted Williams meets Babe Ruth.

SOX (TEMPORARILY) SWEEP ASIDE THE YANKEES

In his first six years as Red Sox owner, Tom Yawkey had used his vast wealth to bring superstars such as Jimmie Foxx, Lefty Grove, and Joe Cronin to Boston and build a contending ballclub. The only thing standing in the way of a pennant now was the New York Yankees, but for a glorious few days even the Bronx Bombers of DiMaggio and Dickey were no match for Yawkey's "Gold Sox."

From July 7 through July 9, 1939, Boston swept five straight games at Yankee Stadium, a spree that highlighted a 12-game winning streak on the road and prompted New York manager Joe McCarthy to quip, "Who the hell are supposed to be the World Champions, us or the Red Sox?" Boston fans hoped for the latter, but by season's end, for the fourth straight October, the Yanks had won it all.

EL TIANTE

Roger Clemens and Pedro Martinez are the two most dominating Red Sox starting pitchers of the past half-century, but for pure entertainment value Luis Tiant still ranks No. 1. Nobody was more adored by his fans or teammates than high-kicking El Tiante, and with a big game to win he was as good as they came.

Possessing a squat, barrel-chested physique and Fu Manchu mustache, the ageless Tiant looked more like a friendly neighborhood mechanic than a big-league star, but he was deceptively athletic and driven to excel. He had stellar baseball bloodlines as the son of a Cuban pitching legend, and he emerged as one of baseball's best hurlers with the Indians in the mid-1960s. Shoulder trouble landed him on the scrap heap by 1971, but the Red Sox took a chance that paid off handsomely. Tiant was 15–6 with a league-leading 1.91 ERA the next year, and from '73 to '76 he went 20–13, 22–13, 18–14, and 21–12 with 18 to 25 complete games per season. His pranks, wisecracks, and ever-present cigar kept the clubhouse loose, and fans loved his enthusiasm and artful, multitudinous deliveries.

When El Tiante smelled a championship, he turned up the heat. He went 11–2 down the stretch in 1972 as Boston fell just short of an AL East title. In the 1975 postseason, he went 3–0, and he threw a two-hitter against Toronto on the final day of the 1978 season to force the one-game playoff with the Yankees. Sadly, that would be his last Red Sox start before signing with the (GASP!) Yanks himself, but he's back where he belongs today, greeting fans with Cuban sandwiches and beer at his El Tiante grill at Fenway.

Stellar Stat: In Game 4 of the 1975 World Series, Tiant had a 5–4 win in which he threw more than 150 pitches for his third complete-game playoff victory in 11 days.

RED SOX TOTALS (1971–78)

W	L	ERA	G	CG	IP	H	ER	BB	SO
122	81	3.36	274	113	1,774.2	1,630	663	501	1,075

MAJOR LEAGUE TOTALS (1964–82)

W	L	ERA	G	CG	IP	H	ER	BB	SO
229	172	3.30	573	187	3,486.1	3,075	1,280	1,104	2,416

MASTER MOTIVATOR

As a utility man on the moribund Red Sox of 1963 and '64, scrappy Dick Williams saw the team's "Country Club" atmosphere of pampered, stat-conscious stars up close. When he took over as Boston's manager three years later, he quickly closed that club.

Williams, just 37, inherited a ninth-place, 72–90 team for 1967 and transformed its attitude virtually overnight—pushing rookies and veterans hard from the start of spring training. The Sox began playing their best fundamental baseball in a generation and added speed to their repertoire. The result was a 100–1 shot that came in: Boston won a thrilling four-team pennant race, and the team very nearly captured a World Series. The future Hall of Famer's tough-guy approach wore thin after three years, but by then it had helped transform the city from second-rate diamond status into Red Sox Nation.

SOX STUMPERS: *The Early Years (1901–1939)*

1. This right-hander won the first home game in Red Sox history. Who is he?

2. What now stands on the site of the team's first ballpark, Huntington Avenue Grounds?

3. Who did the pennant-winning Sox play in the 1904 World Series?

4. Name the three members of Boston's famed outfield during the second decade of the 19th century.

5. Name two of the four future 200-game winners the Red Sox traded to the Yankees between 1918 and 1930.

6. Which Hall of Famer—who was immortalized in verse—managed the last-place Red Sox of 1923?

7. Which infielder paced the American League in stolen bases for the usually slow-footed Red Sox in 1934 and '35?

8. Who did general manager Eddie Collins sign after a particularly fruitful scouting trip to the West Coast in 1936?

Answers

1. Cy Young, who went 33–10 for the 1901 Boston Americans (Red Sox).

2. Northeastern University's Cabot Physical Education Center.

3. Nobody. The New York Giants refused to play the "upstart" American Leaguers.

4. RF Harry Hooper, CF Tris Speaker, and LF Duffy Lewis.

5. Carl Mays, Waite Hoyt, Sad Sam Jones, and Red Ruffing. Hoyt and Ruffing are Hall of Famers.

6. Frank Chance, first baseman on the Cubs of Tinkers-to-Evers-to-Chance fame.

7. Billy Werber, who had 40 steals in 1934 and 29 in '35.

8. Minor-leaguers Ted Williams and Bobby Doerr of the San Diego Padres.

Only Six . . .

Only six players have accumulated 2,000 or more hits while in a Red Sox uniform—Carl Yastrzemski (3,419), Ted Williams (2,654), Jim Rice (2,452), Dwight Evans (2,373), Wade Boggs (2,098), and Bobby Doerr (2,042). Interestingly, only two members of this elite group (Boggs and Rice) ever had 200 hits in a season, although Yastrzemski did lead the American League in hits twice.

BOSTON 1B—OF

CARL YASTRZEMSKI RED SOX

CAPTAIN TEK

When Red Sox fans first saw the captain's *C* on the front of Jason Varitek's uniform jersey back in 2005, many thought it looked pretty silly. Hockey teams traditionally single out their leaders this way, but the letter appeared woefully out-of-place on a baseball shirt—even if Varitek had just been named the first Red Sox captain since Jim Rice.

Over time, however, people got used to the *C*, just as they had grown accustomed to seeing the switch-hitting catcher take command for the Sox on the field. Whether steadying a pitcher, coming up with a clutch hit, or even (when necessary) shoving his mitt in an opposing player's face, Tek did what it took to win. In assessing his value to two world champion teams, statistics are of no real use. Varitek may not have produced like Big Papi or Manny, but he was perhaps the most important player on the '04 and '07 rosters.

Varitek certainly put up decent numbers. His 104 home runs and 412 RBI behind the plate from 2002 to '07 ranked behind only Jorge Posada in both categories among all big-league receivers, and his 11 postseason homers (through 2010) put him in a tie for second in team history. He's also produced at least 30 doubles on five occasions and has earned a Gold Glove for his defensive work. But it's his encyclopedic knowledge of opposing hitters that Sox pitchers claim is his greatest asset; even when his days as a starter ended in 2010, nobody worked harder preparing himself and others for a game. In a word, he's indispensable—*C* or no *C*.

Stellar Stat: Through 2010, Varitek had caught a team record 1,420 games, including four no-hitters—a major league record. Carlton Fisk is second on Boston's longevity list with 990 games behind the plate.

RED SOX/MAJOR LEAGUE TOTALS (1997-2010)											
BA	G	AB	R	H	2B	3B	HR	RBI	SB	OBP	SLG
.258	1,478	4,877	632	1,258	296	13	182	721	25	.343	.436

THE REAL CURSE: BIGOTRY

The Red Sox certainly could have used Babe Ruth during the 1920s and '30s, but letting the Bambino slip away is not what cursed the Red Sox. Guys like Jackie Robinson, Sam Jethroe, and Willie Mays could have called Fenway Park home too, if management had been willing to see past their skin color. Even in the early 1990s, one could count the team's current African American players without using all the fingers of one hand.

They had their chances. In 1945, under pressure from city councilmember Isadore Muchnick and some influential newspaper columnists, the Red Sox gave Negro Leaguers Robinson, Jethroe, and Marvin Williams a tryout at Fenway. Baseball's unwritten color line that kept blacks out of the majors was still in effect, but Tom Yawkey's Sox could have broken through and made history. It wasn't to be. It was later reported that a racial epithet was shouted from a team representative in the stands during the session, and none of the trio heard from the Red Sox again.

Two of them would, however, be heard *from*. Robinson signed on with the Brooklyn Dodgers that fall, and by 1947 this fiery leader was helping Brooklyn to the first in a string of National League pennants. Jethroe emerged a few years later as NL Rookie of the Year for the 1950 Boston Braves, who during this period signed several African American ballplayers. One of those signees was Henry Aaron, and he and his mates helped form a top-notch club that, after moving to Milwaukee, won two pennants and the 1957 World Series.

Although those close to owner Yawkey insist that he was not a racist, his Boston team nevertheless watched the parade of progress go right past its front door. In the late '40s, the Red Sox had a Double-A farm team in Birmingham, Alabama, that shared its ballpark with the Negro Leagues' Birmingham Barons. The Barons offered Sox management a chance to look over their top players before any other big-league club had the opportunity, but Yawkey's crew

L-R: Frank Malzone, Don Buddin, Pumpsie Green, Pete Runnels

didn't think any of them had the "skills" to make it—including a young outfielder by the name of Willie Mays.

Only in 1959, after 25 years of Yawkey ownership that had produced zero World Series championships, did the Red Sox finally field their first two African American players: Pumpsie Green and Earl Wilson. It was progress, to be sure, but the tempo had already been set. Boston, the last major-league club to break the color barrier, was deemed a place black ballplayers were not welcome, by fans and management alike, and it would take more than 40 years, several lawsuits, and the end of the Yawkey regime to change this image. After Ellis Burks came up in the late 1980s and Jim Rice was released, Burks was the only man of his race in Boston's starting lineup. Now *that's* a curse.

MR. TWO-TIMER

How rare is it to win back-to-back World Series as a manager? Consider this: In Boston it's happened just once, when Bill Carrigan turned the trick for the 1915 and 1916 Red Sox.

A Lewiston, Maine, native who played baseball and football at Holy Cross, Carrigan first joined the Sox in 1906 as a catcher and earned the nickname Rough for his fearless playing style. He helped the 1912 club to the World Series title and then took over as player-manager at just 29 years old the following year. Within four seasons he had captured two more championships—helped immensely by a young pitcher he nurtured along named George Herman Ruth.

Carrigan quit at the top after 1916 to go into banking back in Lewiston, but he returned to manage the dismal Red Sox from 1927 to '29—when the team averaged 98 losses per season. Under those circumstances, "Rough" took on a different meaning.

RED-HOT ROOKIES

Tony Conigliaro, 1964

Tony Conigliaro almost slept through his first major-league game. After his second, he must have thought he was dreaming.

A local hero who had grown up a few miles from Fenway Park, Tony C homered high over the Green Monster on the first pitch thrown to him there just a few days after oversleeping and arriving late to Yankee Stadium for the '64 season opener (which was rained out). His tardiness earned the rookie a $10 fine, but the 19-year-old outfielder was wide awake the rest of the year. He slugged the ball with authority, despite missing nearly two months after a Pedro Ramos pitch broke his arm. For the handsome, hard-luck slugger, it was a harbinger of far tougher days ahead.

ROOKIE YEAR TOTALS											
BA	G	AB	R	H	2B	3B	HR	RBI	SB	OBP	SLG
.290	111	404	69	117	21	2	24	52	2	.354	.530

GAME 6—STILL THE BEST?

It was beginning to appear that the conclusion to an intoxicating 1975 Red Sox season would come in the sixth game of the World Series at Fenway Park. Boston's big-game maestro Luis Tiant had been staked to a 3–0 lead over the Reds on Fred Lynn's first-inning home run, but by the top of the eighth Cincinnati had knocked out a tiring El Tiante with six unanswered runs. A chill was in the air; autumn was coming.

Since there had already been several come-from-behind wins in the Series, however, there was hope that the Sox could eke out another one. Two players got on in the Boston eighth, but with two outs, pinch hitter Bernie Carbo looked horrible in barely fouling off ace closer Rawley Eastwick's 2–2 pitch. Some fans were perhaps already adding Ks in their scorecards when Carbo righted his swing on Eastwick's next delivery and sent it over the center-field wall for an implausible three-run homer and a 6–6 tie.

The game remained deadlocked into the 11th when Joe Morgan of the Reds hit his own shot to right that looked like it, too, was going out. Dwight Evans tracked the ball to the right-field corner, and then in an athletic and intuitive three-part play leaped to pluck it out from the seats, spun, and threw it back in toward first base to help double-up stunned baserunner Ken Griffey and end the inning.

It was past 12:30 A.M. when Carlton Fisk led off the bottom of the 12th for Boston, and after taking a ball from Pat Darcy, he sent the reliever's second offering high toward the left-field foul pole. Fisk knew it would be either gone or foul, so he took just a few steps down the baseline and began frantically leaping and waving his arms, willing the ball to stay on the fair side of the pole for a home run. An NBC camera operator situated in the left-field scoreboard kept his lens frozen on Fisk rather than moving to track the ball—he wasn't drawn to the drama of the situation, he'd been startled by a huge rat and thus unintentionally captured what became an iconic image for millions of TV viewers (and millions since on replays). This was punctuated by Fisk's reaction upon seeing the ball clang fair off the pole. Pudge smiled, gave a

final leap and clap, and started around the bases with his Series-tying run.

Boston Globe columnist Ray Fitzgerald suggested the two teams call off the seventh contest after this "Beethoven symphony played on a patch of grass." Unfortunately for Sox fans, a finale *was* waged, but even that excruciating 4–3 loss couldn't erase the good feelings left over from Game 6.

GOOD HANDS

Although the Red Sox have most often been associated with heavy hitting and power pitching, many standout defensive players have made their mark with the club. Before great fielding was officially recognized with the establishment of the Rawlings Gold Glove Awards in 1957, some of the best at flashing leather for the Sox were third baseman Jimmy Collins in the earliest years of the franchise; the outfield trio of Harry Hooper, Tris Speaker, and Duffy Lewis during the 1910s; the double-play combo of second baseman Bobby Doerr and shortstop Johnny Pesky in the '40s; and their teammate in center field, Dom DiMaggio.

Starting with third baseman Frank Malzone in the inaugural Rawlings class of 1957, 17 different Boston players had won at least one Gold Glove in the little more than a half-century of the honor's existence. Dwight Evans, master of Fenway's sun-splashed right field, led the way with eight, while in two seasons—'68 and '79—the team had three recipients. Not all the best slick-fielding Sox earned the honor, however: Rico Petrocelli (shortstop and third base), Alex Gonzalez (shortstop), and Coco Crisp (center field) are a few of the defensive standouts who never earned Gold Gloves with Boston—but might have if Fenway fans were doing the voting.

Dwight Evans

Red Sox Gold Glove Winners (1957–2010)

1. Dwight Evans, RF* 1976, 1978, 1979, 1981, 1982, 1983, 1984, 1985

2. Carl Yastrzemski, LF* 1963, 1965, 1967, 1968, 1969, 1971, 1977

3. Fred Lynn, CF* 1975, 1978, 1979, 1980

4. Frank Malzone, 3B 1957, 1958, 1959

5. George Scott, 1B 1967, 1968, 1971

6. Jimmy Piersall, CF* 1958

7. Jackie Jensen, RF* 1959

8. Reggie Smith, CF* 1968

9. Carlton Fisk, C 1972

10. Doug Griffin, 2B 1972

11. Rick Burleson, SS 1979

12. Mike Boddiker, P 1990

13. Ellis Burks, CF* 1990

14. Tony Peña, C 1991

15. Jason Varitek, C 2005

16. Kevin Youkilis, 1B 2007

17. Dustin Pedroia, 2B 2008

*Although three outfield awards are given annually in each league, they are not specified by LF, CF, or RF; the listings here indicate each player's primary outfield position with the Red Sox.

RED SOX NATION: PRESIDENT REMDAWG

Other teams may have loyal fans, but only Red Sox Nation can claim a president who was sworn in by a justice of the U.S. Supreme Court.

Jerry Remy, the popular Sox broadcaster and former Boston second baseman, was issued his oath of office as president of Red Sox Nation in February 2008 by Justice Stephen Breyer in Washington, D.C. The ceremony followed a popular election the previous fall in which 70,000 die-hards voted by e-mail and postcards for their favorite of five finalists. The RemDawg easily outdistanced Rob "Regular Guy" Crawford, an educator and musician whom Remy then named vice president. More than 160,000 ballots had been cast in earlier run-offs that narrowed down a list of 1,257 initial nominees to 10—or 11, if you include the dog named "Big Pupi."

RICO GOES 6-TO-5

Fondly remembered for catching the final out of the 1967 pennant-clincher, Rico Petrocelli was a productive and popular infielder with the Red Sox through a dozen seasons and two World Series appearances.

The scrappy Brooklyn native was Boston's regular shortstop at age 22 and an All-Star starter in '67 and '69. He hit 40 home runs (then a record for shortstops) in the latter campaign and then followed those up with 29 and 28 blasts the next two years. Shifted to third base with Luis Aparicio's arrival in 1971, Petrocelli continued to excel defensively as his power numbers dropped. And though injuries prompted his early retirement, Petrocelli still hung 'em up ranked fifth on the club's all-time homer and RBI lists.

Stellar Stat: Petrocelli's lifetime fielding percentage ranks among the Red Sox top five at third base (.970) and at shortstop (.969).

RED SOX/MAJOR LEAGUE TOTALS (1963, '65-76)											
BA	G	AB	R	H	2B	3B	HR	RBI	SB	OBP	SLG
.251	1,553	5,390	653	1,352	237	22	210	773	10	.332	.420

TEDDY BALLGAME

Each year the ranks of fans who saw Ted Williams play grow smaller, and today those who remember watching The Kid hit a homer—even when *they* were kids—are all well past 50. Yet as Ted sightings shift from deeply ingrained eyewitness accounts to grainy highlight reels, it appears certain that future generations will still be able to identify the greatest player in Red Sox history.

Statistically, Williams's numbers stack up well against those from any era. The 6′4″, left-handed hitter lost most of five seasons serving in two wars, as well as big chunks of three others due to injury and an aborted retirement. This left just 14 years that he played more than 110 games for the Sox, and within that limited time frame No. 9 led the American League in on-base percentage twelve times; slugging percentage nine times; batting average, runs scored, and total bases six times each; and home runs and RBI on four occasions.

Twice—in 1942 and '47—Teddy Ballgame won the Triple Crown as the AL's batting, home run, and RBI champ, and in '49 he missed a record third when he was edged out by Detroit's George Kell in the batting race, .34291 to .34276. His lifetime on-base percentage is the best in history, and his slugging mark is second only to Babe Ruth. No batter—not Musial, Carew, Brett, or Gwynn—has hit .400 since Ted finished at .406 in 1941. For many years he was closest, checking in at .388 in 1957, the summer he turned 39.

Mere numbers, however, don't tell the full story. The rail-thin teen (hence another nickname, The Splendid Splinter) from San Diego honed his batting talents in a largely loveless household, and hitting became the lonely boy's focus and obsession. As his local legend grew, he also developed a healthy degree of cockiness: Signed away from the Pacific Coast League's San Diego Padres in 1937 by Boston GM Eddie Collins, he was farmed out from his first Red Sox training camp the next spring but let his hecklers know he'd soon be back to out-earn them. He did exactly that, and until his final at-bat four decades later—when, naturally, he homered—Williams was the one player others clamored to watch hit.

Timing identified Ted as both a member of "The Greatest Generation" and of baseball's "Golden Era," and he stood out in both groups. A Marine flight instructor during World War II, he later flew 39 combat missions in Korea and survived a fiery crash landing. He was an expert fisherman, was movie-star handsome, and became a champion for numerous charities—most notably the Jimmy Fund of Boston's Dana-Farber Cancer Institute. His oft-stated desire was to be the greatest hitter who ever lived; on the way to (arguably) achieving it, he wound up being much more.

Stellar Stat: Twice named AL MVP (in 1946 and '49), this future Hall-of-Famer was a close runner-up in voting four times—including both his Triple Crown seasons.

RED SOX/MAJOR LEAGUE TOTALS (1939-42, '46-60)											
BA	G	AB	R	H	2B	3B	HR	RBI	SB	OBP	SLG
.344	2,292	7,706	1,798	2,654	525	71	521	1,839	24	.482	.634

NO LOVE LOST:
THE RED SOX AND THE YANKEES

When Yankees boss Hank Steinbrenner and his staff heard that a construction worker with Red Sox loyalties had buried a David Ortiz replica jersey under the foundation of the new Yankee Stadium in 2008, two men were dispatched to jackhammer through concrete and bring the tattered shirt to the surface. Ortiz himself had never even been near the guilty garment, but Steinbrenner was taking no chances on its bad karma affecting his team.

So it goes with the Red Sox and Yankees. Arguably the two most storied franchises in baseball, they are also the game's fiercest rivals—and their ownership (and fans) will stop at nothing to get an edge. For most of a century it was really no contest; although the Sox won five World Series titles to New York's none through 1918, the tables had been turned since the Yanks purchased a fellow named George Herman Ruth from Boston in January 1920. New York won its first pennant a year later, its first

World Series in 1923, and through 2003 a resounding 26 world championships to Boston's *none* since the Babe hit Manhattan.

Sure, the Red Sox won a few pennants themselves, and in some years—such as 1949, '77, and '78—they gave the Yanks a real run for their money before faltering. But Boston's World Series nightmares gave rise to talk of a "Curse of the Bambino" haunting the franchise. When the wild card playoff format finally enabled the teams to face one another in postseason play, this just meant more disappointment for Boston fans after AL Championship Series losses in 1999 and 2003. It wasn't until their incredible comeback of 2004 that the Sox were finally able to silence the chants of "Ninnnnnneteen-Eigggggghteen!!" at Yankee Stadium, and now it's the Sox who can claim two World Series titles to New York's zero this century. It all means one thing is for sure—where there is Red Sox karma, the Yankees will try to chisel it out.

SHORE BAILS OUT THE BABE—PERFECTLY

Ruth, Shore

Red Sox left-hander Babe Ruth made a handsome living finishing off opponents with his bat and pitching arm. But when he couldn't finish his job one day, a teammate made the most of the situation.

Ruth was gunning for his second straight 20-win season when he faced the Washington Senators at Fenway Park on June 23, 1917. Upon walking leadoff man Ray Morgan, however, the hot-headed lefty had choice words for umpire Clarence "Brick" Owens and was ejected. As policemen and Sox manager Jack Barry dragged Ruth off the field, right-hander Ernie Shore calmly replaced him. Morgan was promptly thrown out trying to steal, and Shore retired the next 26 batters in a 4–0 win. Officially ruled a no-hitter, it was as near a perfect game as you can get—and the greatest relief job in history.

> **" Once more a Boston team had arisen in its might and preserved a reputation never smirched in the post-season contests for the big stakes. "**
>
> — PAUL SHANNON, THE *BOSTON POST*, WHEN RED SOX WON THE
> 1918 WORLD SERIES—THEIR FIFTH IN FIVE TRIES SINCE 1903

RED-HOT ROOKIES
Walt Dropo, 1950

On the popular Baseball-Reference.com Web site, Walt Dropo's statistical page is sponsored by "The kids" in honor of "Grandpa Walter." Hopefully it makes him smile when he sees it; otherwise, one could easily imagine the former Red Sox first baseman shuddering as he looked past the "1950" line.

For that one season, Dropo was pure dynamite. The 6′5″, 220-pound "Moose from Moosup" (Connecticut) set a still-standing team record for home runs by a first-year player and finished just one RBI short of teammate Ted Williams's major-league rookie mark. Throw in his high average, and you not only had the AL Rookie of the Year, you had a guy primed for years of stardom—that is, until he suffered Boston's worst-ever sophomore slump with a .239 average, 11 homers, and 57 ribbies in 1951. Shortly thereafter, the Moose was vamoosed—to Detroit.

ROOKIE YEAR TOTALS											
BA	G	AB	R	H	2B	3B	HR	RBI	SB	OBP	SLG
.322	136	559	101	180	28	8	34	144	0	.378	.583

BEFORE BROOKS

Overshadowed by the likes of Ted Williams and Jackie Jensen in Boston's lineup and later by Brooks Robinson in American League Gold Glove voting, Frank Malzone was nonetheless a standout hitter and third baseman.

Army duty delayed his ascent to the majors, but as a 27-year-old rookie in 1957 Malzone batted .292 with 103 RBI. His average season was more in the solid .280, 15-homer, 80-ribbie range, and defensively the six-time All-Star was rivaled in the AL only by Robinson and later Clete Boyer. Malzone did manage to win three Gold Gloves before Brooksie clamped down on the honor in 1960, and he remained one of the league's best contact hitters throughout his career.

Stellar Stat: Malzone led all AL third basemen in games played, putouts, assists, errors, double plays, and fielding percentage as a rookie, and in one 1957 contest he had a record ten assists.

RED SOX TOTALS (1955-65)											
BA	G	AB	R	H	2B	3B	HR	RBI	SB	OBP	SLG
.276	1,359	5,273	641	1,454	234	21	131	716	14	.317	.403
MAJOR LEAGUE TOTALS (1955-66)											
BA	G	AB	R	H	2B	3B	HR	RBI	SB	OBP	SLG
.274	1,441	5,428	647	1,486	239	21	133	728	14	.315	.399

What If...?

Red Sox history, especially that which transpired during the 86-year World Series title drought, can largely be encapsulated in a series of questions that fans have pondered through the decades from their seats in living rooms, bars, and Fenway Park. So, what if...

Owner Harry Frazee had hung on to Babe Ruth for one more year—and he hit 54 homers?

Minor-leaguer Pee Wee Reese had not been sold to the Dodgers?

The Red Sox had signed Jackie Robinson and/or Willie Mays when they had the chance?

Ted Williams hadn't suffered an elbow injury in an exhibition game held just before the 1946 World Series?

Joe McCarthy had started Parnell or Kinder instead of Denny Galehouse?

Harry Agganis had lived?

Jackie Jensen hadn't been afraid of flying?

Bernie Carbo had still been around to pinch-hit against the Yankees in '78's one-game playoff instead of Bob Bailey?

Dave Stapleton had gone in for Bill Buckner toward the end of Game 6 in the '86 World Series?

The Sox had hung on to minor-leaguer Jeff Bagwell instead of trading him for reliever Larry Anderson?

PARK

PEDRO POWERS PAST THE INDIANS AND CLEMENS

Capping a fantastic first season for the Red Sox, Pedro Martinez saved two of his best performances for last—and trumped a former Boston ace in the process.

On October 11, 1999, in the fifth and deciding game of the American League Division Series against Cleveland, Martinez came on in relief during the fourth inning after Bret Saberhagen and Derek Lowe were chased. He had a sore back that had forced him from Game 1, but the score was tied at 8 apiece, and there was no tomorrow for the loser. So challenged, Pedro proceeded to pitch six hitless innings with eight strikeouts as the Red Sox won 12–8. Judging by his grin as teammates carried him from the field after their first playoff series victory since 1986, he didn't mind the pain at all.

Next up for the Sox were the Yankees in the American League Championship Series, and Martinez's Game 3 opponent at Fenway was none other than his predecessor as Boston's ace hurler—free-agent deserter Roger Clemens. Newspapers hyped the October 16 match-up as "Cy Young" vs. "Cy Old," but the projected duel for the ages turned into a laugher as the Sox shelled Clemens for five runs on six hits in just two innings while backing Pedro with 21 hits in a 13–1 victory. Martinez went seven, giving up just two hits and notching 12 strikeouts. Fans heckled their hero-turned-villain with chants of "Roooooooger! Roooooooger!" as he left the mound, but the good karma didn't last—New York still won the series in five games.

1912 WORLD SERIES

In terms of the last millennium, 1912 was the perfect Red Sox season. After inaugurating Fenway Park with a win, Boston put together a 105–47 record—still its most victories ever—and cruised to the pennant. Fireballer "Smoky" Joe Wood (34–5) and center fielder Tris Speaker (a .383 average and showstopping defense) delivered off-the-charts production, and the Sox didn't face a real challenge until the World Series.

Led by legendary manager John McGraw and pitching ace Christy Mathewson, the New York Giants recovered from a three-games-to-one Series hole to force an eighth and deciding game (one contest had ended in a tie). The finale at Fenway was an instant classic. Mathewson held a 1–0 early lead, but Harry Hooper kept the Red Sox close by diving into the right-field stands to steal a home run from Larry Doyle. Boston tied it in the seventh on a pinch-double by Olaf Henriksen, and there it remained until the tenth. The Giants scored, but the Red Sox answered and then got one more thanks to two botched fly balls and Larry Gardner's title-winning sacrifice fly.

Classic Kernel: Game 7 at Fenway was delayed for nearly 30 minutes when Boston's "Royal Rooters" fan contingent marched onto the field in protest after finding its regular right-field seats occupied.

CHAPTER FIVE

SO THIS IS WHAT IT FEELS LIKE

"*I dreamt about this day. I said my prayers every night to the big guy: 'Bring us a World Series.'*"

—JOHNNY PESKY, OCTOBER 27, 2004

Pitcher Mike Timlin and friends celebrate the 2004 World Series victory.

THE GREY EAGLE SOARS

Long before the likes of Jackie Jensen, Reggie Smith, and Nomar Garciaparra arrived on the scene, Tris Speaker was a five-tool player capable of taking control of a game for the Red Sox with his glove, bat, speed, and smarts.

As a center fielder, the Grey Eagle had an astounding 196 assists from 1909 through 1915, including 35 in both 1909 and 1912. His approach, which gained him fame throughout baseball, was twofold: Knowing that few players had the capacity to crush the ball where he couldn't run it down, he played close enough to the diamond that he almost served as a fifth infielder by grabbing line drives and racing across the second base

bag for unassisted double plays. When batters did smack balls deep, however, he raced back with seemingly effortless strides and grabbed them over his shoulder—then spinning and using his terrific arm, he'd often throw out those trying to advance.

Defense was only part of Speaker's game. As a left-handed batter, the solidly built six-footer may have been the greatest Red Sox hitter prior to Ted Williams, routinely finishing among American League leaders in batting average, doubles, triples, home runs, RBI, and stolen bases. Although he did pace the circuit in homers once for Boston, two-base hits were his true forte—as his major-league record of 792 doubles attests. His Sox batting average is third behind Williams and Wade Boggs in team history, and despite playing just seven full seasons in the Hub, he also ranks second all-time in triples and stolen bases for Boston.

Speaker's best friend and roommate was pitching ace Joe Wood, and the pair led the Red Sox to the World Series title in Fenway Park's debut year of 1912 when Speaker hit .383 and Wood went 34–5. The Sox won it all again in 1915, but Speaker didn't get along well with manager Bill Carrigan due to the religious cliques then prevalent on the team (Speaker was Protestant; Carrigan, Irish Catholic). Team president Joe Lannin, who wanted to cut Speaker's salary from $18,000 to $9,000 after his batting average fell to .322 over three years, was another enemy, and Speaker became trade bait after irking his two bosses further by holding out after Lannin's lowball offer. Just before Opening Day 1916, fans were shocked to learn that the Grey Eagle had been sold to the Indians for $50,000, pitching prospect Sad Sam Jones, and infielder Fred Thomas.

The Red Sox won two more world championships in the next three years without Speaker, but they certainly could have used him over the next 13 seasons—which he spent primarily with Cleveland amassing the gaudy lifetime totals that ensured his inclusion among the first dozen players selected for the Baseball Hall of Fame.

Stellar Stat: In 1912, when he won the Chalmers Award (equivalent to today's MVP), Speaker had 222 hits, 136 runs scored, 53 doubles, 12 triples, and 52 steals to go along with his .383 average and league-high 10 home runs.

RED SOX TOTALS (1907–15)											
BA	G	AB	R	H	2B	3B	HR	RBI	SB	OBP	SLG
.337	1,065	3,935	704	1,327	241	106	39	542	267	.405	.482
MAJOR LEAGUE TOTALS (1907–28)											
BA	G	AB	R	H	2B	3B	HR	RBI	SB	OBP	SLG
.345	2,789	10,195	1,882	3,514	792	222	117	1,529	432	.428	.500

Fenway Factoids

The same day Fenway Park opened (April 20, 1912), Tiger Stadium was unveiled in Detroit. When the latter ballpark closed after the 1999 season, Fenway officially became the oldest venue in the majors.

Before fire codes made overcrowding illegal, 47,627 bloated Fenway for a Sox-Yankees doubleheader in 1935. (The park's current capacity is close to 40,000.)

For many years a bowling alley open to the public ran underneath Fenway. When it was dismantled, wood from the alley was used to build a bar inside the ballpark.

It was tough to tell who the players were at Fenway even *with* a scorecard until the Red Sox first added numbers to their uniforms in 1931.

Boston College, Boston University, and the Boston (now New England) Patriots all played football at Fenway for various periods. Other nonbaseball events held there include soccer matches, hockey games, a Franklin Roosevelt campaign speech, and concerts by Bruce Springsteen and the Rolling Stones.

Lights were added to Fenway in 1947, and the first video message board debuted in 1976, but the hand-operated scoreboard has remained in continuous use since the first game.

The stretch of Jersey Street passing by Fenway's main entrance was renamed Yawkey Way in 1976 to honor longtime Sox owner Tom Yawkey. The park's official address is now 4 Yawkey Way.

On September 8, 2008, the Red Sox set an MLB record for most consecutive home game sellouts with 456. Extending it to 600 on July 18, 2010, the team kept the streak open into 2011.

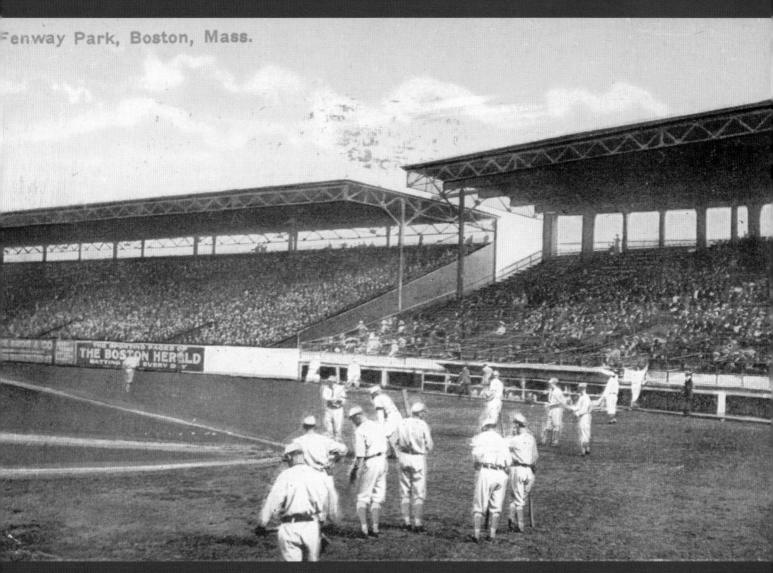

Fenway Park, Boston, Mass.

THE SPORTING PAGES OF
THE BOSTON HERALD
BATTING ... EVERY D Y

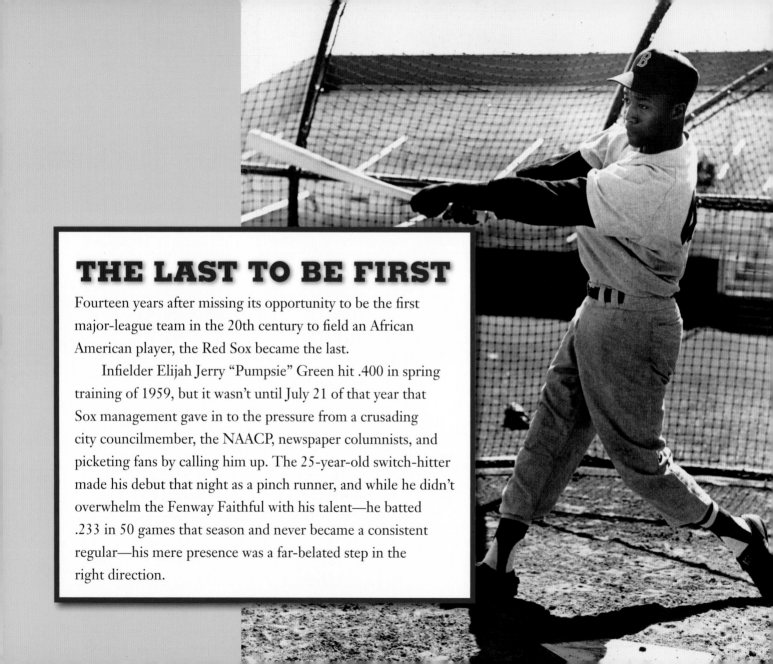

THE LAST TO BE FIRST

Fourteen years after missing its opportunity to be the first major-league team in the 20th century to field an African American player, the Red Sox became the last.

Infielder Elijah Jerry "Pumpsie" Green hit .400 in spring training of 1959, but it wasn't until July 21 of that year that Sox management gave in to the pressure from a crusading city councilmember, the NAACP, newspaper columnists, and picketing fans by calling him up. The 25-year-old switch-hitter made his debut that night as a pinch runner, and while he didn't overwhelm the Fenway Faithful with his talent—he batted .233 in 50 games that season and never became a consistent regular—his mere presence was a far-belated step in the right direction.

FIRST LADIES OF THE SOX

Lolly Hopkins

Women have embraced baseball in large numbers since the "Ladies Days" of the 19th century, but few fans of either gender can match the devotion of Red Sox rooters Lolly Hopkins and Elizabeth "Lib" Dooley.

The widow of a train conductor, Hopkins rode the rails up from Rhode Island regularly from the 1930s through the '50s to attend games at Fenway and Braves Field. She had an entourage known as "Lolly's Girls" and was famous for tossing Tootsie Rolls to her favorite players and cheering them through a megaphone—hence her nickname, "Megaphone Lolly."

Dooley, a Boston schoolteacher, had season tickets at Fenway for 55 years—they were in the first row of Box 36-A between the home on-deck circle and the dugout. A close friend of Ted Williams, Lib missed only a handful of 4,000 home games through mid-1999 and had business cards that proclaimed her "A Friend of the Red Sox." She doled out Starbursts and Oreos to her heroes, and Williams called her "the greatest Red Sox fan there'll ever be." After her June 2000 death, she was buried with the game ball from that day's Sox-Yankees battle.

MAKING A CASE FOR RICE

Even when compared with today's inflated offensive numbers, Jim Rice's stats—especially during his prime years of 1977 through 1979—jump off the page. Just look to your right.

Back when far fewer players reached 20 homers or 100 RBI, Rice routinely topped these totals. Excluding the strike of 1981, Jim Ed averaged a 28-dinger, 110-ribbie season from 1975 to 1986—not coincidentally, Boston's only two pennant-winning campaigns in a 36-year span. He hit the ball hard and often, blasting tape-measure homers and scorching line drives. Twice, he even had 15 triples—an almost unfathomable total for a power hitter with average speed.

Sure, he hit into a lot of double plays, and while his defense in left field improved tremendously over time, he never made folks forget his predecessor, Carl Yastrzemski. But this quiet South Carolinian was the best pure hitter in a lineup of All-Stars and was acknowledged as a great teammate who played hurt and never complained. Pitchers feared his coming to the plate, and despite a reputation for being aloof, sportswriters respected him—the 1978 MVP, he finished in the top five in voting five other times. A rapid decline starting at age 34 (reportedly due to deteriorating vision) cost him the "magic" lifetime numbers of .300 and 400 homers that help earn entrance into the Hall of Fame, but in 2009 he finally received the call to Cooperstown—and saw his number 14 retired by the Red Sox.

Stellar Stat: Rice's 406 total bases in 1978 made him the first (and last, so far) AL player to exceed the 400 mark since Joe DiMaggio in 1937.

STEAMING RICE							
Year	Runs	Hits	HR	RBI	BA	SLG	TB
1977	104 (4)	206 (3)	**39 (1)**	114 (3)	.320 (6)	**.593 (1)**	**382 (1)**
1978	121 (2)	**213 (1)**	**46 (1)**	**139 (1)**	.315 (3)	**.600 (1)**	**406 (1)**
1979	117 (3)	201 (2)	39 (2)	130 (2)	.325 (4)	.596 (2)	**369 (1)**
(AL rank in parentheses/bold if leader)							

From the Cyclone to the Rocket

ALL-TIME VICTORIES

T1. Cy Young.................................192
   (team-record 38 shutouts)

T1. Roger Clemens 192
   (also 38 shutouts!)

3. *Tim Wakefield 179

4. Mel Parnell 123

5. Luis Tiant 122

T6. Joe Wood 117

T6. Pedro Martinez......................117

8. Bob Stanley 115

9. Joe Dobson 106

10. Lefty Grove 105

*Through 2010

SINGLE-SEASON VICTORIES

1. Joe Wood *34–5 1912

2. Cy Young.......... *33–10 1901

3. Cy Young.......... *32–11 1902

4. Cy Young.......... *28–9 1903

5. Cy Young.......... 26–16........... 1904

T6. Wes Ferrell....... *25–14 1935

T6. Dave Ferriss.........25–6........... 1946

T6. Mel Parnell........ *25–7 1949

T9. Babe Ruth 24–13 1917

T9. Roger Clemens *24–4 1986

*Led American League

The week after his enshrinement at Cooperstown, Jim Rice had his number retired at Fenway Park on July 28, 2009. Like all major-league teams, the Red Sox also retired Jackie Robinson's No. 42 in 1997.

1 — Bobby Doerr
4 — Joe Cronin
6 — Johnny Pesky
8 — Carl Yastrzemski
9 — Ted Williams
14 — Jim Rice
27 — Carlton Fisk
42

Only Seven...

Only seven of the more than 1,500 men to play for the Red Sox have had their uniform numbers retired by the club. They are immortalized atop the right-field grandstands at Fenway Park, along with an eighth athlete who never wore a Boston jersey but could have, if not for the narrow-mindedness of the day.

1986 WORLD SERIES

It doesn't hurt nearly as much to think about it anymore. The title years of 2004 and 2007 have in large part exorcised the demons of World Series past, and looking back to the seven-game setbacks of '46, '67, '75, and even '86 has become less an act of masochism and more one of healthy introspection for Red Sox fans. It's like a recovering alcoholic recalling the days of his or her worst benders; as great as things are going now, it never hurts to reflect on where you've been.

The 108–54 Mets were heavy favorites in the 1986 Series until the Sox captured the first two contests on the road. New York turned the tables at usually friendly Fenway, but things still looked good for Boston when Bruce Hurst gutted out a second win and Cy Young Award–winner/MVP Roger Clemens was on tap for Game 6. Clemens had a 3–2 lead and a four-hitter through seven innings, but he developed a blister and...well, you know what happened next, right? The Mets tied it in the eighth, but Boston went up by two in the tenth before New York won on a three-run, two-out rally in the bottom of the tenth. That only allowed New York to *tie* the Series, but the Red Sox fell in the seventh game.

See? That wasn't so bad, was it?

Classic Kernel: Boston's implosion overshadowed outstanding Series performances by second baseman Marty Barrett (a .433 average on 13 hits) and Hurst (2–0, 1.96 ERA).

Jim Rice scores in Game 5.

ALL-STARS OLD AND NEW SHINE AT FENWAY

In a contest billed as the ultimate All-Star Game that saw baseball's greatest living stars assembled at Fenway Park, it would appropriately be two Red Sox who made the most-lasting impressions at the 1999 mid-summer classic.

Before the July 13 game, as Aaron, Mays, Feller, and the rest of the "All-Century Team" watched from the Fenway diamond, ailing Red Sox icon Ted Williams was driven in from center field to home plate in a golf cart. Teary-eyed, he waved while riding past the crowd, and a long standing ovation continued as the 80-year-old—nearly blinded by two strokes—walked with help to the mound. There fellow batting champ Tony Gwynn steadied him for a ceremonial first pitch to Red Sox great Carlton Fisk, and superstars from Musial to Griffey clamored to shake Ted's hand.

It took several awkward attempts by an announcer imploring, "Will the legends of baseball please leave the field?" before the throng around Williams finally dispersed and Sox ace Pedro Martinez could take the hill as the American League starter. Not wanting to be outdone by the old-timers, he proceeded to strike out five National League batters over two innings—Barry Larkin, Larry Walker, Mark McGwire, Sammy Sosa, and Jeff Bagwell—without allowing a hit. The AL won 4–1, Pedro was the MVP, and Williams added a final notch to his legend.

"Hell, I haven't had a base hit in 30 years, and I'm a better hitter now than I've ever been in my life."

—TED WILLIAMS AT THE 1999 ALL-STAR GAME

Ted Williams, surrounded by (l-r)
Cal Ripkin, Jr.; Juan Marichal; and Frank Robinson

VOICES OF THE SOX
FROM GOWDY TO TODAY

"Howdy, neighbor, have a 'gansett." Repeat these words to most Red Sox fans over a certain age, and they will likely evoke memories of hot summer nights spent listening to legendary broadcaster Curt Gowdy describe another home run for Teddy Ballgame over the airwaves while slipping in a plug for Narragansett Beer.

It's the same with "Way back! Waaaaay back!" or "Can you believe it?!" in recent years. Any Sox aficionado old enough to reach a Fenway turnstile likely recognizes the trademark radio calls of Jerry Trupiano and Joe Castiglione, and with tickets to Yawkey Way now far more difficult and expensive to acquire, tuning in to games remains a very popular pastime—especially with streaming audio on the Internet connecting folks from around the world.

It doesn't even matter if the team is any good. When the Red Sox were struggling through years of mediocrity (or worse) in the 1950s and '60s, Gowdy kept things entertaining with great insights and an engaging voice. The 1967 Impossible Dream team will never be forgotten, but neither will the wonderful work of its "voices"—Ken Coleman and Ned Martin. Coleman even turned his calls from that year into a best-selling album, and he was still around when the '86 Sox won the pennant.

Under blankets at home and summer camp, countless fans formed lifelong loyalties to the Sox through Coleman's familiar, friendly descriptions of the action. Today, whether it's longtime vet Castiglione exclaiming his disbelief over a wild play or one of the team's Spanish broadcasters at the microphone, the tradition continues.

Curt Gowdy

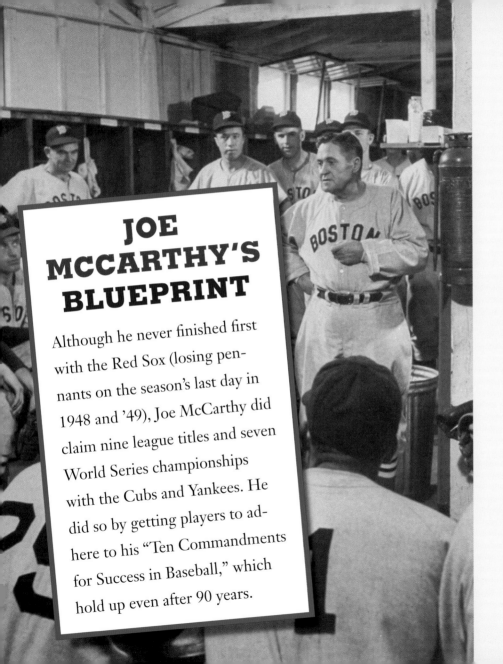

JOE MCCARTHY'S BLUEPRINT

Although he never finished first with the Red Sox (losing pennants on the season's last day in 1948 and '49), Joe McCarthy did claim nine league titles and seven World Series championships with the Cubs and Yankees. He did so by getting players to adhere to his "Ten Commandments for Success in Baseball," which hold up even after 90 years.

1. Nobody ever became a ballplayer by walking after a ball.

2. You will never become a .300 hitter unless you take the bat off your shoulder.

3. An outfielder who throws in back of a runner is locking the barn after the horse is stolen.

4. Keep your head up and you may not have to keep it down.

5. When you start to slide, slide. He who changes his mind may have to change a good leg for a bad one.

6. Do not alibi on bad hops. Anybody can field the good ones.

7. Always run them out. You can never tell.

8. Do not quit.

9. Do not fight too much with the umpires. You cannot expect them to be as perfect as you are.

10. A pitcher who hasn't control hasn't anything.

RED-HOT ROOKIES

Carlton Fisk, 1972

He exploded across the Boston baseball landscape in '72, moving from third string to the starting lineup in a month and never looking back. The kid from New Hampshire hit for average and power, steadied a young pitching staff, chided star team-mates Reggie Smith and Carl Yastrzemski for not hustling, and led the Red Sox on a charge for the AL East title that fell a half-game short. A Septem-ber *Sports Illustrated* cover boy, he led the league in triples, finished second in slugging, and earned a Gold Glove. Not surprisingly, he was the American League's first unanimous Rookie of the Year, and he finished fourth in MVP voting.

ROOKIE YEAR TOTALS

BA	G	AB	R	H	2B	3B	HR	RBI	SB	OBP	SLG
.293	131	457	74	134	28	9	22	61	5	.370	.538

FENWAY'S GREATEST GAME

Five hours and 49 minutes of taut, do-or-die drama featuring two bitter rivals, two Hall of Fame starting pitchers, 30 left on base, a capacity crowd of 35,120 hanging on every one of 471 pitches, and four-and-a-half scoreless extra innings before a winner could be decided. With all due respect to Game 6 of the 1975 World Series, Game 8 of the 1912 fall classic, and the one-game playoff between the Red Sox and Yankees in 1978, the best contest in Fenway history has to be the fifth game of the 2004 American League Championship Series waged between these same two clubs on October 18, 2004.

Still down three to one in a best-of-seven Series, even after David Ortiz's 12th-inning homer early that same morning had sealed Game 4, the Sox gave the ball to ace Pedro Martinez in what would be his last start at Fenway in a Boston uniform. Pedro held a 2–1 lead over New York starter Mike Mussina until the sixth, when Yankees shortstop Derek Jeter hit a two-out, three-run double off Martinez that silenced the raucous crowd. The Sox were on the fringe of elimination again, but they tied it in the eighth as Ortiz homered against Tom Gordon and Jason Varitek's sacrifice fly off a suddenly mortal reliever Mariano Rivera plated Dave Roberts.

From that point on, the teams traded jabs like two great prizefighters—putting players on base but failing to get them home—until Ortiz came up in the bottom of the 14th with two on and two outs. After a succession of foul balls, Big Papi hit a blooper off Esteban Loaiza that landed in center field to give Boston the victory and sent the Sox back to New York with all they could ask for, a chance.

Johnny Damon scores the winning run and is met by Doug Mientkiewicz at home plate.

THE BEST THERE EVER WAS...OCTOBER 18, 2004

						R	H	E
New York	010	003	000	000	00	4	12	1
Boston	200	000	020	000	01	5	13	1

KKKKLEMENS KS 20—AGAIN!

Many fans complained that Roger Clemens was "dogging it" during his last four mediocre (40–39) years in Boston, but late in the 1996 season the free-agent candidate showed he was still capable of dominating.

After starting the year 4–10, Clemens had won five of six when he took the mound at Detroit on September 18. He struck out nine men over the first four innings as Boston took a 3–0 lead, and it soon became clear that Clemens had a shot at his own record of 20 whiffs in a nine-inning game. Even Tigers fans were cheering him on, and when Travis Fryman swung and missed the Rocket's 151st and last pitch, Clemens had matched his 1986 masterpiece: 20 strikeouts, zero walks. Unfortunately for Red Sox fans, he'd have only two more starts in a Boston uniform.

Whether it was a desire for more free-agent leverage or just his talent shining through, Clemens made a dramatic turnaround his final two months in a Red Sox uniform.

Roger Clemens, 1996	W	L	ERA	CG	IP	SHO	BB	SO
First 23 starts	4	10	4.13	2	159	0	74	164
Last 11 starts	6	3	2.69	4	83.2	2	32	93

PICK A SEAT, ANY SEAT

Trying to get a hot dog at Fenway Park today often means navigating oneself around hordes of fans at and near the concessions stands. Those seeking refreshments on September 28–29, 1965, had no such problem. On those two days, the moribund Red Sox—mired in ninth place in the American League—drew only 461 and 409 spectators, respectively, to their 35,000-seat ballpark for meaningless late-season games with the California Angels.

Boston's lineup featured two great young hitters, Tony Conigliaro and Carl Yastrzemski, and September 28 starter Dave Morehead had pitched a no-hitter at Fenway just two weeks before. But years of losing and uninspired play had taken their toll, and Tom Yawkey's ballpark—and ballclub—was in dire need of a lift. Both would get it two years later.

"*I threw so hard I thought my arm would fly right off my body.*"

—JOE WOOD, ON STRIKING OUT NEW YORK GIANTS ART FLETCHER AND DOC CRANDALL TO END GAME 1 OF THE 1912 WORLD SERIES; WOOD WON HIS FIRST OF THREE VICTORIES IN THE SERIES BY THE SCORE OF 4–3.

"*Can I throw harder than Joe Wood? Listen, mister, no man alive can throw any harder than Smoky Joe Wood.*"

—WALTER JOHNSON, 417-GAME WINNER AND 12-TIME STRIKEOUT CHAMPION, DURING WOOD'S 34–5 SEASON IN 1912.

Only Eight...

In the long, lead-footed history of the Red Sox (through 2010), only eight players have stolen 35 or more bases in a season for Boston—and just three of them have turned the trick since Franklin Roosevelt's first term. Jacoby Ellsbury's 70 thefts in 2009 stands as the team record, breaking Tommy Harper's longstanding mark of 54 set in 1973. Besides these two, Otis Nixon (42 in '94) is the only other man to crack 35 since Billy Werber led the league with 40 in 1934.

SMOKY JOE DERAILS THE BIG TRAIN

The newspapers billed it, Joe Wood fondly remembered, like a heavyweight title fight. The young Red Sox pitcher entered his September 6, 1912, matchup against Washington Senators ace Walter Johnson on a 13-game winning streak. Johnson had won a record 16 straight earlier in the same campaign and was baseball's top strikeout artist.

Fenway Park was so crowded that some overflow fans were seated directly on the field along the first- and third-base lines, with the players occupying benches in front of them. The contest lived up to their expectations, with the Red Sox scoring the game's only run on back-to-back doubles by Tris Speaker and Duffy Lewis in the sixth. Wood, who pitched a six-hitter with nine strikeouts, eventually tied Johnson's string of 16 consecutive victories en route to a 34–5 record and a World Series title.

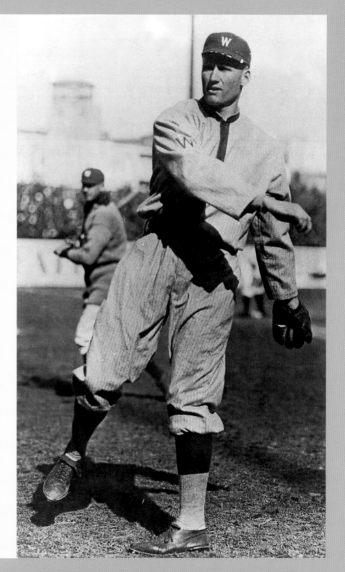

RED SOX TOTALS (1954–59, '61)

BA	G	AB	R	H	2B	3B	HR	RBI	SB	OBP	SLG
.282	1,039	3,857	597	1,089	187	28	170	733	95	.374	.478

MAJOR LEAGUE TOTALS (1950–59, '61)

BA	G	AB	R	H	2B	3B	HR	RBI	SB	OBP	SLG
.279	1,438	5,236	810	1,463	259	45	199	929	143	.369	.460

JACKIE JENSEN, GOLDEN BOY

Along with Harry Agganis's death and the team's failure to move forward on integration, Jackie Jensen's premature retirement at age 32 was a key reason Boston fell to the bottom of the American League in the early 1960s. Jensen was a five-tool player who starred with Ted Williams in Boston's outfield, but the quiet slugger quit at the height of his career due to a terrible fear of flying.

A standout in baseball and in football as an All-American halfback at the University of Southern California, Jensen played with the Yankees and Senators before coming to Boston in 1954. A fast, sure-handed right fielder, he was also an offensive force—leading the league in RBI in 1955, '58, and '59 while hitting 20 to 30 homers per season. He was not the prototypical plodding Sox slugger either; his 22 stolen bases in '54 paced the junior circuit, as did his 11 triples two years later.

With his boyish face, cropped blond hair, and football-hardened frame, the man the press dubbed Golden Boy resembled Yankees superstar Mickey Mantle—and in 1958 he succeeded Mantle as American League MVP after a 35-homer, 122-ribbie summer. Jensen put up similar numbers in '59 (and won a Gold Glove) but then abruptly retired because of his flying phobia. He did try coming back a year later but quit for good after a so-so 1961 season (.263, 13 homers) on a miserable team. His lifetime totals of 199 home runs, 929 RBI, and 143 steals were impressive given his brief tenure (1,438 games), but they also teased of what could have been.

Stellar Stat: Jensen averaged 111 RBI a season from 1954 through '59, during which he led the majors with 667.

One and Done

*Many players have had outstanding first seasons with the Red Sox and then failed
to stay on top for one reason or another. Here are just a few of them:*

Rookie **Buck O'Brien** was a 20-game winner for the 1912 World Series champs, but he started 1913 with a 4–9 slate and was sold to the White Sox for $5,000.

Dale Alexander batted .372 in 1932 after a June trade from Detroit and led the league with a .367 overall mark; the next year he hit .281 and suffered a knee injury that when improperly treated led to gangrene, and his big-league career was over.

Rudy York had 119 RBI in 1946 plus two game-winning home runs in the World Series, but early the next year he was swapped to the White Sox with a .212 average after nearly burning down a hotel room with an errant cigarette.

First baseman **Walt Dropo** was the 1950 Rookie of the Year with a .322 average, 34 homers, and 144 RBI; he fell off to .239, 11, and 57 the next year and was traded to the Tigers early in '52.

Don Schwall also earned Rookie of the Year honors with a 15–7 record in 1961, but after a 9–15 sophomore campaign he was sent packing for Pittsburgh.

After 1969 rookie **Mike Nagy** went 12–2 with a 3.11 ERA at age 21, he struggled to a 7–8 mark in parts of three more years with Boston.

Denny Doyle batted .310 and had a 22-game hitting streak for the pennant-winning '75 Sox after a June trade from California; he played two more seasons in Boston, hitting .250 and .240.

New center fielder **Carl Everett** was a .300 hitter with 34 home runs in 2000, but he checked in with a lackluster .257 mark and 14 dingers a season later—then was checked out to Texas.

Carl Everett

Don Schwall

Denny Doyle

SCHILL THE THRILL

He may have talked too much for some people's taste, but few athletes could back up their words like Curt Schilling.

The big right-hander promised a championship when he joined the Red Sox in November 2003, and he delivered the next October—24 wins and two bloody socks later. When folks whispered he was done after an injury-plagued 2007, he begged to differ—then came on again in the postseason as the Sox claimed their second World Series title in his four seasons with the team. Schilling was by no means a solitary hero in the resurgence, but his 6–1 playoff record for Boston makes one thing clear: He'll never have to pick up a tab in the city again.

Stellar Stat: Schilling's 21–6 regular season in 2004 made him just the eighth pitcher to win 20 his first year with the Red Sox and the first since Dennis Eckersley in 1978.

"If there was ever a man born to be a hitter it was me."
—TED WILLIAMS

"He gave us pride. I got to see Ted from the time he broke into baseball, and he was just a dynamic, different type of a guy. I've always compared him to a General Patton— dominating people."

—BOBBY DOERR

BOBBY DOERR:
SOLID AT SECOND

He lacked the magnetism of Ted Williams, the sheer power of Jimmie Foxx, and the famous lineage of Dom DiMaggio. Soft-spoken Bobby Doerr sought no fanfare as he suited up every day, but his excellence on the field and his class and leadership off it earned him distinction from lifelong friend Williams as "the silent captain of the Red Sox." These attributes also gained him a spot in the Hall of Fame.

A Los Angeles native who grew up playing ball with past and future big-leaguers, Doerr was a .342 hitter for the Pacific Coast League's San Diego Padres when the Red Sox snatched him up (along with teammate Williams) in 1936. Just 19 the next spring, Doerr made Boston's roster and went 3-for-5 on Opening Day. An April beaning curtailed his playing, but he was Boston's starting second baseman when 1938 began. Other than his time in the service during World War II, he'd hold the job for the next 13 years.

Doerr progressed rapidly, driving in 80 runs his second season and batting .318 in 1939. By 1940, still only 22, he had his first big power year with 22 homers and 105 runs batted in. He'd eventually top the 100 RBI mark six times, rare production at the time for a middle infielder, and he shined defensively as well—often leading the league in double plays, assists, and putouts on the way to retiring with a then-record .980 fielding percentage. Recognized with nine All-Star selections from 1941 to '51, he started five midsummer classics and had a three-run homer to help the AL to victory in 1943.

Initially rejected for army duty in World War II because he had both a young son and a perforated eardrum, Doerr was finally accepted and ordered to report in September 1944. The timing possibly cost him the MVP Award, as he was batting .325 with a league-leading .528 slugging mark, but after missing all of the '45 season he returned in fine form—knocking in 116 runs and leading the league in every key defensive category for the 1946 pennant-winning Red Sox. Batting .409, he led Boston's regulars in the World Series against St. Louis, but the Sox lost in seven.

Because he debuted so young, it has been largely forgotten that Doerr's career ended prematurely. After batting .294 with a career-high 27 homers, 120 RBI, and 11 triples in 1950, he suffered a serious back injury the following summer and had to quit for the season in August. Warned that surgery could worsen the problem, he chose to retire altogether to his Oregon farm at age 33—but he did get a chance to don a Red Sox uniform again as first-base coach with the fabled "Impossible Dream" team of 1967.

Stellar Stat: Doerr is the only Red Sox player to hit for the cycle twice—on May 17, 1944, and May 13, 1947. In the latter game, both his single and double came in the eighth inning.

RED SOX/MAJOR LEAGUE TOTALS (1937–44, '46–51)											
BA	G	AB	R	H	2B	3B	HR	RBI	SB	OBP	SLG
.288	1,865	7,093	1,094	2,042	381	89	223	1,247	54	.362	.461

THREE TOUGH LOSSES

The Red Sox have had their share of heartbreaking setbacks through the years, but only in a few cases has genuine tragedy befallen the team.

Outfielder Chick Stahl, named player-manager of the club in November 1906, was apparently distraught from marital troubles the following spring training when he drank carbolic acid in his hotel room. He died within minutes due to massive internal hemorrhaging. Ed Morris, a big, boozing pitcher for the Sox, was stabbed at a fish fry just before spring training in 1932 and died from an infection picked up after diving in a lake for a swim getaway. Stahl was 34 years old; Morris 32.

A generation later, in 1955, local boy-made-good Harry Agganis of Lynn was hitting over .300 as a Sox first baseman when he was hospitalized with a severe cold and chest pains. Pneumonia developed, and after initially rallying, the Golden Greek suddenly died on June 27 of a pulmonary embolism. A wake for the 26-year-old first baseman and former football All-American from Boston University drew approximately 10,000 mourners, more than many games at Fenway that sad summer.

*The Red Sox and the Washington Senators
pay their respects to Harry Agganis at
Washington's Griffith Stadium.*

RED-HOT ROOKIES

Jonathan Papelbon, 2006

With only eye-popping statistics and old movie footage to go on, it was hard for people under age 40 to understand just how dominating a reliever Dick Radatz had been for the Red Sox in the early 1960s. Then they saw fist-pumping Jonathan Papelbon and his darting 94 mph fastball, and they realized what the old-timers were talking about.

A 6'4" fan favorite, "Pap" was Radatz redux during the '06 season. Unscored upon in his first 14 appearances, he allowed just one run over his first 33 games, and by season's end he had compiled the eighth-lowest ERA ever for a pitcher throwing 50 or more innings. The right-hander held batters to a .167 average, tying Pedro Martinez's 2000 club record, and was just the second Sox rookie pitcher to ever be named an All-Star.

ROOKIE YEAR TOTALS

W	L	ERA	G	CG	IP	H	R	ER	BB	SO
4	2	0.92	59	0	68.1	40	8	7	13	75

FRED LYNN:
THE ROOKIE MVP

Tumbling catches in center field. Leaping grabs against the Green Monster. The sweetest left-handed swing this side of Ted Williams. Hollywood handsome, with a genuine good-guy demeanor, Fred Lynn had it all, and for a while he seemed destined for Cooperstown.

The first rookie to be named MVP (when he led the Red Sox to the 1975 World Series), this laid-back Californian was an All-Star each of his six full seasons in Boston and earned four Gold Gloves. He peaked with a batting title (.333), 39 homers, and 122 RBI in 1979, but he was never the same hitter after being traded to the Angels a year later.

Stellar Stat: While a Red Sox, Lynn hit .350 with a .608 slugging percentage in 412 games at Fenway Park.

RED SOX TOTALS (1974–80)

BA	G	AB	R	H	2B	3B	HR	RBI	SB	OBP	SLG
.308	828	3,062	523	944	217	29	124	521	43	.383	.520

MAJOR LEAGUE TOTALS (1974–90)

BA	G	AB	R	H	2B	3B	HR	RBI	SB	OBP	SLG
.283	1,969	6,925	1,063	1,960	388	43	306	1,111	72	.360	.484

Boston's Pinch Thomas catches behind Brooklyn's Hy Myers in Game 2.

1916 WORLD SERIES

In a ritual that was becoming old hat to their players and fans, the Red Sox suited up for their third World Series in five seasons—this time against the Brooklyn Robins (who would not officially take on their more familiar *Dodgers* moniker until 1931). Boston's lineup was packed with poised veterans hardened from postseason experience, and it showed.

During the Series opener, the Sox held off a furious Brooklyn rally in the ninth, as the visitors got four runs and loaded the bases with two outs before shortstop Everett Scott's diving stop in the hole and throw to first beat Jake Daubert by a half-step to end it. Boston's 23-game-winner Babe Ruth was the story in Game 2, pitching a 14-inning complete game that concluded on a pinch-hit by Del Gainer as darkness descended on Braves Field (where the Sox played their World Series home games in 1915 and '16 because it could accommodate more paying customers than could their own Fenway Park).

The Robins raced to an early lead in the third contest at Ebbets Field, and this time Boston made the late comeback that fell one run short. But Brooklyn couldn't maintain its momentum: Boston captured the next two games for the title, including a Columbus Day clincher at home before the city's biggest-ever postseason crowd—42,620.

Classic Kernel: Although they hit just two home runs in the Series (both by Larry Gardner), the Red Sox had a record six triples.

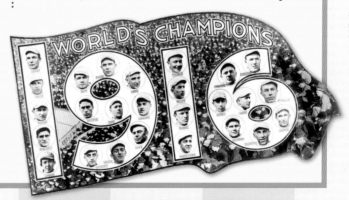

HENDU PROVIDES THE SPARK

Before the 1986 Red Sox let a world championship vanish from their grasp, they performed a much more pleasing Houdini act in the American League Championship Series—sparked by an unlikely yet very likable hero.

Dave Henderson was a fourth outfielder picked up from the Seattle Mariners for the '86 stretch run, but while "Hendu" brought an engaging personality to Boston, his bat was initially silent. He hit just .196 the remainder of the regular season and entered Game 5 of the ALCS against the California Angels only after starting center fielder Tony Armas sprained his ankle. The Sox trailed three games to one in the best-of-seven series and were facing elimination on the road.

In the bottom of the sixth, with Boston ahead 2–1 and a man on second, Angel Bobby Grich hit a deep shot to center; Henderson timed it right with a leaping catch against the padded fence, but the impact jarred the ball out of his glove and over the wall for a hard-luck home run. California now led 3–2 and had stretched the advantage to 5–2 when Boston came up in the ninth. A Bill Buckner single and Don Baylor homer made it 5–4, and when Angels pitcher Gary Lucas hit Rich Gedman with two outs, ace closer Donnie Moore was brought in to face a final (they hoped) batter: Henderson.

Hendu worked the count to 2 and 2, fouled off several Moore fastballs, and then sent a splitter far over the left-field fence for a 6–5 Boston lead. His hop, skip, and jump and ear-to-ear grin while watching the ball sail out remains one of the top video clips in Sox history. And while the Angels initially rebounded to tie the game, Henderson came through again with a game-winning, 11th-inning sacrifice fly.

The Sox still trailed the series three games to two, but the devastating loss and the hardship of traveling 3,000 miles to Fenway Park for Games 6 and 7 seemed to unnerve the Angels. Boston easily won the last two contests, 10–4 and 8–1, to seal both the pennant and Hendu's permanent spot alongside Bernie Carbo in the Red Sox Hall of Role-Player Heroes.

Josh Beckett

TROUNCING THE TRIBE

The opponent was different, but the results were the same for the Red Sox in the 2007 American League Championship Series—another big hole, another great comeback.

After historically erasing a three-games-to-none deficit to beat the Yankees in the 2004 ALCS, the Sox merely had to overcome a three-games-to-one lead by the Indians in the '07 playoffs. Cleveland had won three straight after Boston took the opener and hoped to clinch at home behind eventual Cy Young Award–winner C. C. Sabathia. But Sox ace Josh Beckett hurled his second gem of the series to top Sabathia 7–1 in Game 5, and back at Fenway, Boston trounced the Tribe in Games 6 (12–2) and 7 (11–2) to win its 12th pennant and a World Series berth with the red-hot Colorado Rockies.

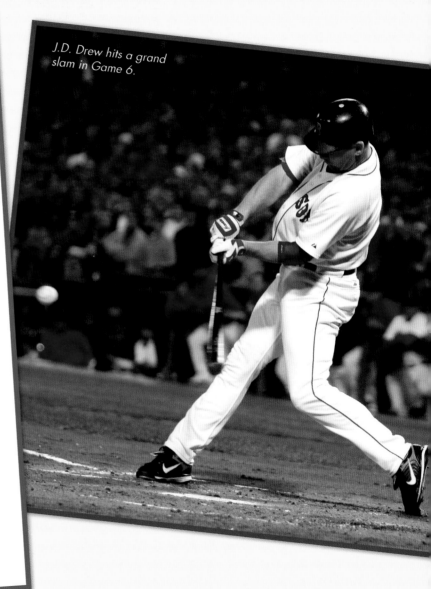

J.D. Drew hits a grand slam in Game 6.

TED AND YAZ

One succeeded the other, No. 9 followed by No. 8. Carl Yastrzemski took over in left field for the Red Sox in 1961, the spring after Ted Williams vacated the spot. He may have initially resented being labeled as an "heir apparent" to The Kid, but Williams helped Yaz through a frightful rookie slump. And if Yaz never quite lived up to Williams's class as a hitter or headline maker, he was a pretty good runner-up—and nobody, including Williams, could play Fenway's left-field wall better. By the time Captain Carl retired in 1983, he and Williams were side by side atop the Red Sox all-time lists in hits, runs, home runs, RBI, doubles, and fan adulation.

"I know—I know all about you. Look kid, don't ever—ya understand me?—don't ever let anyone monkey with your swing."

—Williams to Yastrzemski on seeing him hit for the first time

"He studied hitting the way a broker studies the stock market and could spot at a glance mistakes that others couldn't see in a week."

—Yastrzemski on Williams

Williams and Yastrzemski

CHAPTER SIX

CARDIAC KIDS AND IMPOSSIBLE DREAMS

"The game begins in the spring, when everything else begins again, and it blossoms in the summer, filling the afternoons and evenings, and then as soon as the chill rains come, it stops and leaves you to face the fall alone."

—BART GIAMATTI, FROM "THE GREEN FIELDS OF THE MIND"

Fans welcome a new season.

THE WATCH OF '79

Although Carl Yastrzemski needed only 131 hits entering the 1979 season to reach 3,000 for his career—a mark then attained by just 13 big-league players—the "Yaz Watch" didn't begin in earnest until Captain Carl's 400th career home run at Fenway Park on July 24. His game-winning shot off Oakland A's hurler Mike Morgan left him 39 hits shy of his target, and with 68 games left in the season, the speculation began as to when the veteran outfielder would reach the historic milestone.

By September, with the slumping Red Sox dropping out of contention in the AL East, tracking Yastrzemski's progress became the central focus of each game for Sox fans. Today folks would be checking PDAs or cell phones every five minutes for cyber-updates, but back then they needed to watch or listen to the games. If they missed one or were out of broadcast range, they could try to catch the nightly news, call in to the *Boston Globe*'s 24-hour sports hotline, or check the *Globe*'s "Yaz Watch" box on the top front-page corner of each day's sports section.

For a while the big, bold "hits to go" numbers in the *Globe* box were descending daily—15, 13, 12, 11—but then the weary, 40-year-old Yastrzemski went cold at the plate. Boston had a six-game home stand in early September, and everybody wanted him to reach 3,000 at Fenway. After collecting No. 2,999 against the Orioles on September 9, however, Yaz went 0-for-12 over his next three games against Baltimore and the Yankees. Finally, in the eighth inning on September 12, in his last at-bat before the Sox hit the road, he grounded a Jim Beattie pitch just under New York second baseman Willie Randolph's outstretched glove. The single made him just the fourth player after Stan Musial, Willie Mays, and Henry Aaron to achieve both 400 homers and 3,000 hits—and the first American Leaguer to do so.

> *"I know one thing. The last hit was the hardest of all 3,000. It took so long because I really enjoyed all those standing ovations you gave me the last three nights."*

— CARL YASTRZEMSKI,
SEPTEMBER 12, 1979

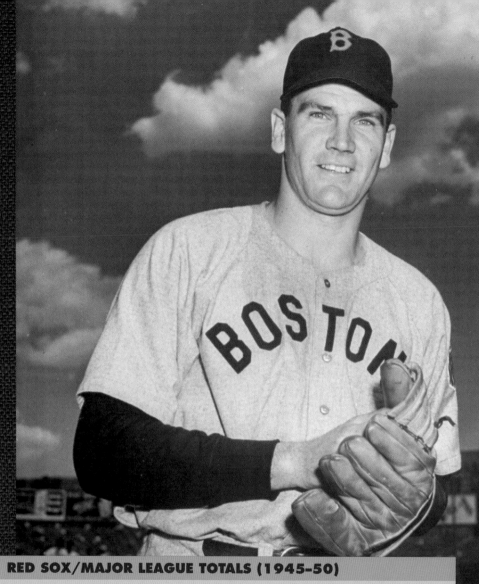

RED SOX/MAJOR LEAGUE TOTALS (1945–50)

W	L	ERA	G	CG	IP	H	R	ER	HR	BB	SO
65	30	3.64	144	67	880	914	392	356	42	314	296

FERRISS WAS FLEETING

His shoulder betrayed him at a young age, but before it did, David "Boo" Ferriss was briefly one of the best pitchers in Red Sox history—and one of the top hurlers in the American League, as well.

A native of tiny Shaw, Mississippi (his nickname came from his toddler expression for "brother"), he was signed by the Red Sox out of Mississippi State in 1942 and shortly thereafter entered the Army Air Corps. The 6'2" right-hander played service ball with numerous big-leaguers, and upon being discharged due to asthma in early 1945, he was sent right up to aid Boston's war-depleted staff. Three of his first four starts were shutouts, and he soon reached 8–0 with wins over all seven American League foes. Fans packed Fenway for his remaining games, and he wound up 21–10 with a 2.96 ERA for a seventh-place team.

There was some speculation as to how Ferriss would fare once the "big boys" returned in 1946, but he did just fine: A 25–6 record gave him the league's best win-loss percentage (.806), which he paired with a 3.25 ERA for the American League champs. He hurled a six-hit shutout in Game 3 of the World Series against St. Louis but allowed three runs over 4⅓ innings in Boston's Game 7 loss. Ferriss's shoulder injury came in '47, when the club's "Big Three" of Boo, Tex Hughson, and Mickey Harris all developed serious arm woes. Ferriss went 12–11 that summer and hung on for pieces of three more seasons before a minor-league odyssey that eventually brought him back to Fenway as pitching coach from 1955 to '59.

Stellar Stat: After loading the bases on walks in his first big-league inning, Ferriss got out of the jam and notched 22⅓ straight scoreless frames to start his career.

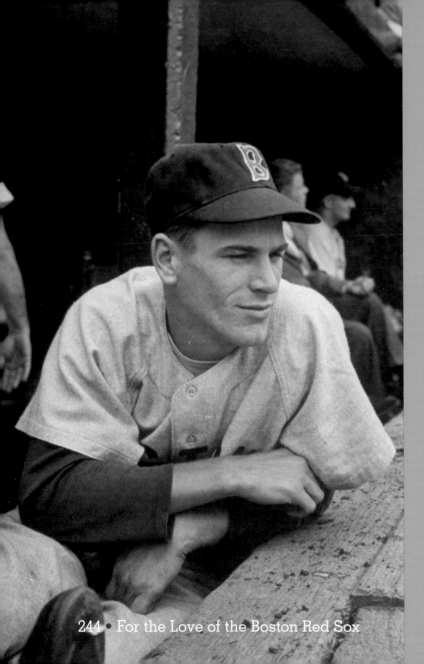

THE UTILITY CHAMP

Batting champions are usually the most feared hitters in a team's lineup, but in 1950 it was a challenge just getting Billy Goodman into Boston's lineup. The regular first baseman for most of 1948 and '49, Goodman was dislodged the next spring by rookie slugger Walt Dropo. Goodman's defense, however, proved as versatile as his bat was valuable. The Red Sox had stellar talent at almost every position, but managers Joe McCarthy and Steve O'Neill kept finding places to plug Goodman in due to injuries—and by year's end he had enough plate appearances to win the batting title with a .354 average.

BILLY GOODMAN'S 1950 MATH

Outfield:	45 games
Third base:	27 games
First base:	21 games
Pinch hitter:	11 games
Second base:	5 games
Shortstop:	1 game
	= 110 games/batting title

THE KID NEARLY DOES IT AGAIN

Although the Red Sox had fallen from contention by 1957, one man on the roster who was aging like fine wine offered up a taste of 1941 vintage that summer.

Ted Williams batted .340 with 22 home runs in the first half of the '57 season, not bad for a guy about to turn 40. What he accomplished after the All-Star break, however, was astounding. Hitting .533 during a 17-game hitting streak, he brought his average up near .400—a mark that no batter had ended a season with since his own .406 in 1941. A severe chest cold slowed him shortly after his August 30 birthday, but then in late September he got hot again to finish with 38 homers and a .388 average—just five hits short of .400.

NEAR MISSES (PART II)

The Red Sox World Series drought had passed 50 years
by the time the 1970s rolled around, a decade in which
Boston had rosters filled with stars but wound up with little
to show for them.

In 1972, for instance, the Sox had future Hall of Famers Carl Yastrzemski, Carlton Fisk, and Luis Aparicio in
their everyday lineup, but a freak incident derailed their
AL East Division title hopes. Boston led the Tigers by
one-half game going into a final three-game set at Detroit,
but usually sure-footed Aparicio slipped rounding third
base in the opener and Yastrzemski (going for a triple)
failed to see him; when both wound up on third, Yaz was
tagged out to help kill a key rally in a 4–1 loss. Detroit won
again the next night, clinching the title. The Sox wound up
one-half game back.

Two years later, Boston's '74 club led the East by
seven games on August 23 and appeared in command. But
a miserable batting slump and eight straight losses the next
week wiped out the lead, and the Sox finished third, seven
games behind division-winning Baltimore.

The 1975 Red Sox revived their crestfallen fans with
a spectacular pennant-winning season, marred only by
a Game 7 loss in the World Series to Cincinnati's "Big
Red Machine." But after a down year in '76, the Sox were
back to their near-miss ways in 1977 as the most powerful
lineup in team history blasted a club-record 213 homers
yet lacked pitching depth and finished 2½ games behind
the champion Yankees.

It had been a rough few years, but the worst was yet
to come.

STILL STANDING

In May 1999, seeking to raise revenue, the Red Sox released plans for a new double-decked venue to replace tiny, outdated Fenway Park. Although "retro" ballparks such as Camden Yards have been very well received, traditionalist Boston fans rallied against this change. "Save Fenway" stickers appeared everywhere, and after purchasing the Sox in 2002, the team's new ownership group announced three years later that they would nix rebuilding plans and continue expanding and enhancing the existing ballpark instead.

This was actually the second time Fenway avoided the wrecking ball. Midway through the 1967 season, after several years of dismal ballclubs and dwindling attendance, then-owner Tom Yawkey announced intentions to sell the Red Sox unless the city financed a new stadium. When his surprising '67 club kept winning, however, Fenway started filling up, and talk of its demise stopped.

STARS LIGHT UP FENWAY

The first half of the 1946 season was an out-of-this-world experience for Red Sox fans, so it seemed only appropriate that they see the stars come out at Fenway Park.

On July 9, as Boston sat in first place with a stellar 54–23 record, Fenway hosted its first major-league All-Star Game. The home team's success was reflected by the American League roster, which featured eight Red Sox players: starters Ted Williams (LF), Dom DiMaggio (CF), Bobby Doerr (2B), and Johnny Pesky (SS), reserves Hal Wagner (C) and Rudy York (1B), and pitchers Boo Ferriss and Mickey Harris. None afforded themselves better in the AL's 12–0 romp than Williams—who went 4-for-4 with five RBI and two homers, one off the arching "eephus" pitch of Pittsburgh's Rip Sewell.

All-Stars (l-r) Boo Ferriss, Rudy York, Bobby Doerr, Hal Wagner, Johnny Pesky, Ted Williams, Mickey Harris, and Dom DiMaggio

1967 WORLD SERIES

If ever a postseason felt anticlimactic, this was the one. The frenetic American League pennant race in which four teams dueled to the final week and a champion was left undecided until the last game had left Red Sox fans emotionally drained. Their young club's rapid ascension from ninth place in 1966 to its first AL title in 21 years was thrilling enough; taking on the vaunted, seasoned St. Louis Cardinals in the World Series three days later was icing on a cake that didn't need any.

Oddsmakers expected the inexperienced "Impossible Dream" Sox to be overmatched, but they silenced the skeptics. St. Louis ace Bob Gibson's dominance and the offensive output of Cardinals Lou Brock, Julian Javier, and Roger Maris proved formidable, but Boston's Jim Lonborg and Carl Yastrzemski carried their club as they had all year right up until the seventh game. Gibson's extra rest before the finale likely made the difference—Lonborg had just two days off to Gibby's three—but Sox players and fans seldom reflect on how the '67 season ended. This time, the joy was in the journey.

Classic Kernel: In his typical gambler fashion, Boston manager Dick Williams started a pitcher in Game 6 with just two big-league victories—and Gary Waslewski came through with 5⅓ solid innings during Boston's final victory.

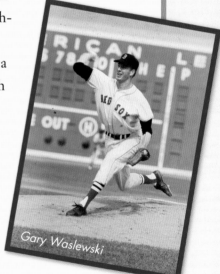

Gary Waslewski

A rare miss for Yaz in the '67 Series.

Smead Jolley

WHAT GOES UP...

One of the quirkiest features of Fenway Park in its early decades was the steep ten-foot embankment that rose in front of the left- and center-field fences. Dubbed "Duffy's Cliff" to honor the skill with which Red Sox left fielder Duffy Lewis traversed it from 1910 to 1917, it proved a much bigger challenge for one of his successors.

Smead Jolley was an excellent hitter for the Sox of 1932 and '33 but was a terrible defensive player who could never master Duffy's Cliff. Once, the story goes, he descended the embankment while tracking a fly ball and fell flat on his face. Reaching the dugout at inning's end, he yelled to his coaches, "For ten days you teach me how to go up the hill, but none of you have the brains to teach me how to come down."

MONSTER'S BALL

The Red Sox were dismal from 1962 through '64, but fans hung around Fenway Park late into games just to see if "The Monster" would emerge from the bullpen. Dick Radatz stood 6′5″, appeared well above his listed weight of 235 pounds, and had a fastball as intimidating as his physique. He fizzled out quickly, but for those three years he may have been baseball's best pitcher, striking out 487 over 414 innings while allowing just 292 hits. In All-Star play, he fanned 10 in 4⅔ frames.

1962	Red Sox.......76–84.....4.22 team ERA	Radatz....... 9–6 ...... 24 saves ..... 2.24 ERA
1963	Red Sox.......76–85.....3.97 team ERA	Radatz...... 15–6 ..... 25 saves ..... 1.97 ERA
1964	Red Sox.......72–90.....4.50 team ERA	Radatz...... 16–9 ..... 29 saves ..... 2.29 ERA

Lonborg's bunt

FROM BUNT TO BUNTING

Although Red Sox sluggers such as Carl Yastrzemski, Tony Conigliaro, and George Scott all contributed numerous key hits during the 1967 Impossible Dream pennant race, the team's most powerful weapon that summer was arguably a dribbler off the bat of a pitcher with a .135 batting average.

On October 1, Sox ace Jim Lonborg was trailing Dean Chance and the Minnesota Twins 2–0 in the final game of the regular season at Fenway Park. The teams were tied atop the American League standings; whoever won might be facing the St. Louis Cardinals in the World Series three days hence. (A one-game playoff between the winner of this game and the Detroit Tigers the next afternoon was also a possibility if the Tigers won their game later that day.) Chance had been virtually unhittable, but then Lonborg, leading off the bottom of the sixth, noticed something as he approached the plate.

"I had bunted a lot during the course of the year, and could run pretty well for a big guy," Lonborg later recalled. "[Cesar] Tovar seemed back a little further at third base than normal, and I had an opportunity on the first pitch to lay one down. Tovar couldn't handle it, and that just started things off."

As a capacity crowd chanted, "Go! Go! Go!," the next three batters all singled—with Yastrzemki's shot to center scoring Lonborg and Jerry Adair to tie the game. A few botched grounders and wild pitches followed, and Boston had a 5–2 lead. Lonborg held on for a 5–3 victory and was carried off on the shoulders of his teammates while thousands of pennant-starved fans mobbed their heroes in what broadcaster Ned Martin accurately called "pandemonium on the field." After Detroit lost to California a few hours later, the Sox were World Series–bound for the first time since 1946.

Darrell Johnson

John McNamara

Grady Little

THE FALL GUYS

Darrell Johnson, John McNamara, and Grady Little each took the Red Sox to the cusp of big-game glory as managers, but in the end bad decisions forever doomed them to Boston's Hall of Shame.

Johnson's 1975 club had reached Game 7 of the World Series against heavily favored Cincinnati when Johnson pinch-hit for veteran reliever Jim Willoughby in the eighth inning of a 3–3 game. The move left rookie Jim Burton on the mound for the ninth, and Joe Morgan made him pay with a Series-winning RBI single. Second-guessers haunted Johnson until his firing a half-season later.

McNamara's '86 Sox held a 5–3 lead over the Mets in Game 6 of the World Series with two outs and nobody on in the 10th. When the game ended five batters later with a ground ball skipping through first baseman Bill Buckner's injury-riddled legs as New York's winning run scored, the manager was roasted. Pundits believed that rather than subbing Dave Stapleton for Buckner, as he had in the late, late innings of Boston's six previous postseason wins,

McNamara had eschewed the defensive switch so the veteran Buckner could bask in the team's on-field victory celebration (which, of course, never came). Even if there were some honorable intentions behind such a decision, fans didn't think it worth the risk. "Knife the Mac" became a popular refrain until his dismissal in mid-1988.

Little's undoing was even more maddening, because while Buckner's gaffe was only partly responsible for the '86 meltdown, Grady's decision directly led to disaster. The Sox led the Yankees 4–2 after seven innings in Game 7 of the 2003 AL Championship Series, and tiring ace Pedro Martinez had a pitch count of exactly 100—the point at which his effectiveness had dropped off all season. Little had a superb bullpen at his disposal, but he left Martinez in for 23 more pitches and four hits (three doubles) in the eighth as the Yanks tied it, 5–5. Ownership wanted Grady fired even before Boston lost the game and series in the 11th, and a few days later they got their wish.

Dustin Pedroia

AL Rookies of the Year

Walt Dropo, 1B 1950

Don Schwall, P.................... 1961

Carlton Fisk, C................... 1972

Fred Lynn, CF 1975

Nomar Garciaparra, SS 1997

Dustin Pedroia, 2B 2007

RED-HOT ROOKIES
Babe Ruth, 1915

He had gotten his feet wet by tossing 23 innings for Boston the year before, but in 1915 George Herman Ruth really began showing the baseball world some of his many gifts.

The unencumbered left-hander, then 20 and barrel-chested, helped the Red Sox win the World Series for the second time in four years. Among American League hurlers, only teammate Dutch Leonard allowed fewer hits per nine innings than Ruth's 6.86, and the rookie even beat Senators great Walter Johnson during the campaign. While management had not yet conceived of playing Ruth in the outfield on off-days, he hinted of his slugging abilities with a .315 average and the first four home runs of his career. There would be plenty more pitching victories—and 710 more homers—to come.

	ROOKIE YEAR TOTALS								
W	L	ERA	G	CG	IP	H	ER	BB	SO
18	8	2.44	32	16	217.2	166	59	85	112

DOMINICAN DANDY

Slight of stature but huge on talent, Pedro Martinez was baseball's most dominant pitcher since Sandy Koufax while in his prime with the Red Sox. His peak years were regretfully short, and injuries often led the team to handle him like fine china, but the exuberant right-hander electrified Fenway like few before or since.

Martinez, a native of the Dominican Republic, was listed at 5′11″ and 170 pounds but was likely much lighter. By age 20 he had joined big brother Ramon (a 20-game winner) on the Dodgers, but manager Tommy Lasorda felt Pedro lacked the strength and size to be successful. He traded him to the Montreal Expos two years later, and there Pedro started to excel. In fact, he became so good that the cash-strapped Expos knew they could never afford to re-sign him; in November 1997, after a Cy Young Award and a year before he could become a free agent, they traded the 26-year-old hurler to Boston.

From Opening Day 1998, when he had 11 strikeouts in a 2–0 win, Martinez became the Prince of Fenway. The white and red K cards popularized during the Boston reign of Roger Clemens came out again, this time adorned with Dominican flags, to begin tally-ing "Punchados de Pedro." There were 251 that first summer, along with a 19–7 record and 2.89 ERA that earned him runner-up status in Cy Young voting. But Martinez, now signed to a lucrative long-term contract, was just warming up.

During 1999 and 2000, he won back-to-back Cy Youngs. In '99, despite a midseason shoulder injury, he was 23–4 with a 2.07 ERA and 313 strikeouts; his ERA was nearly three runs below the league average, and he could barely see runners-up David Cone (3.44 ERA) and Chuck Finley (200 Ks) in his rearview mirror. His 1.74 ERA in 2000 was so far ahead of runner-up Clemens (at 3.70) that it was almost comical. Only a rash of bullpen breakdowns kept Pedro from another 20-win season, but even at 18–6 he was without peer.

Martinez alone couldn't get the Red Sox past the Yankees in the playoffs, and when he was out much of 2001 with tendonitis, they failed even to make the postseason. In '02 he was back with a 20–4 record, but as other strong hurlers such as Derek Lowe and Curt Schilling emerged in Boston, the team began to use Pedro more carefully. In 2003 and '04 this meant less-gaudy records of 14–4 and 16–9, but it also meant he was sufficiently rested for the '04 postseason—when he helped bring home the World Series with a stellar Game 3 victory that was his last in a Red Sox uniform.

Stellar Stat: In what many consider his greatest game, Martinez struck out 17 in a 1-hit, complete-game victory at Yankee Stadium on September 10, 1999—when the Yankees were in the midst of winning three straight World Series.

RED SOX TOTALS (1998–2004)									
W	L	ERA	G	CG	IP	H	ER	BB	SO
117	37	2.52	203	22	1,383.2	1,044	387	309	1,683
MAJOR LEAGUE TOTALS (1992–2009)									
W	L	ERA	G	CG	IP	H	ER	BB	SO
219	100	2.93	476	46	2,827.1	2,221	919	760	3,154

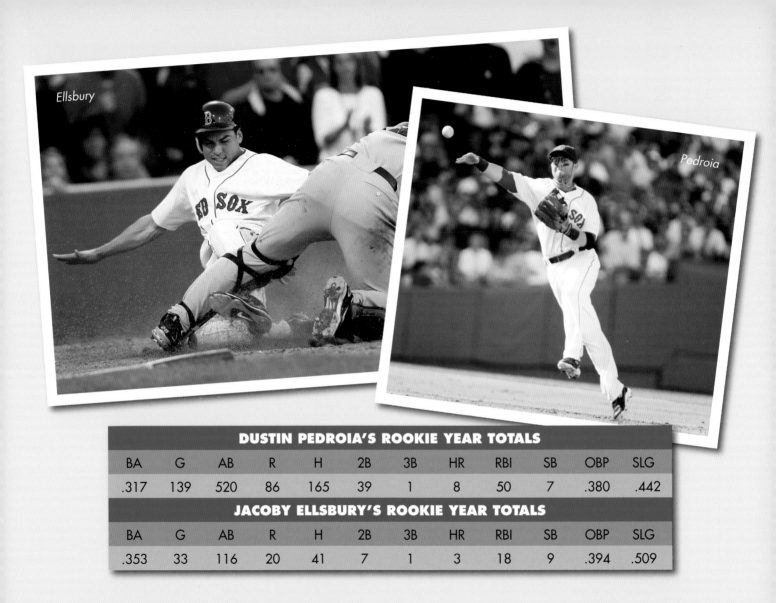

Ellsbury

Pedroia

DUSTIN PEDROIA'S ROOKIE YEAR TOTALS											
BA	G	AB	R	H	2B	3B	HR	RBI	SB	OBP	SLG
.317	139	520	86	165	39	1	8	50	7	.380	.442
JACOBY ELLSBURY'S ROOKIE YEAR TOTALS											
BA	G	AB	R	H	2B	3B	HR	RBI	SB	OBP	SLG
.353	33	116	20	41	7	1	3	18	9	.394	.509

RED-HOT ROOKIES

Dustin Pedroia and Jacoby Ellsbury, 2007

Neither was a factor in Boston's stellar start, but by the time October '07 rolled around, Dustin Pedroia and Jacoby Ellsbury had played a big role in helping the Red Sox gain their first outright American League East title in 12 years.

The 5'9" Pedroia, who had won over doubters throughout his collegiate and minor-league career, earned the second-base job in spring training but endured a horrid 5-for-48 slump over his first month in the majors. He was batting .172 on May 1, with talk-show squawkers calling for his head, but manager Terry Francona left him in, and Pedroia soon silenced his critics with a torrid stretch that raised his average to .315 in just six weeks.

His defense went from steady to spectacular, and his bat stayed strong the remainder of the year. Fenway fans came to love him, due largely to his .351 average at home.

Ellsbury, in contrast, was a can't-miss kid who lived up to the hype. After joining the big club very briefly on two earlier occasions, the team's top-rated prospect was with Boston for the entire September stretch and hit .361 with 17 RBI during the month. His speed, tales of which had preceded him to town, was on display with 9-for-9 stolen bases and outstanding range in left and center field. He and Pedroia were both playing their best ball as the regular season ended—and the best was yet to come.

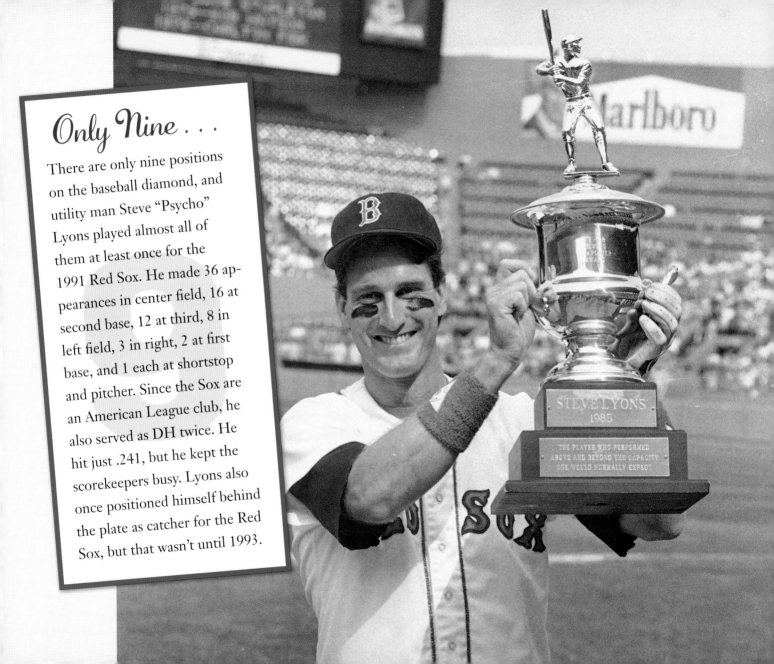

Only Nine . . .

There are only nine positions on the baseball diamond, and utility man Steve "Psycho" Lyons played almost all of them at least once for the 1991 Red Sox. He made 36 appearances in center field, 16 at second base, 12 at third, 8 in left field, 3 in right, 2 at first base, and 1 each at shortstop and pitcher. Since the Sox are an American League club, he also served as DH twice. He hit just .241, but he kept the scorekeepers busy. Lyons also once positioned himself behind the plate as catcher for the Red Sox, but that wasn't until 1993.

STEVE LYONS
1985

THE PLAYER WHO PERFORMED
ABOVE AND BEYOND THE CAPACITY
ONE WOULD NORMALLY EXPECT

SOX STUMPERS: *The Modern Years*

(1980s-Present)

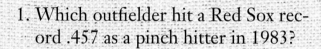

1. Which outfielder hit a Red Sox record .457 as a pinch hitter in 1983?

2. Which pitcher was second in victories behind Roger Clemens on the 1986 Red Sox?

3. Who hit for a slumping Jim Rice in 1988, a move that resulted in a confrontation between Rice and manager Joe Morgan?

4. For the first time in 18 years, the 1992 Red Sox did not have a hitter with 20 home runs. Who led Boston in homers that year?

5. Clemens was the first non-outfielder since 1938 to win an MVP award with the Red Sox. Who was the second?

6. Which pitcher in the Red Sox bullpen converted a then-record 43 straight saves in 1998?

7. Derek Lowe and Pedro Martinez gave the 2002 Red Sox something they had not had since 1949. What was it?

8. Name five of the eight players on both the 2004 and 2007 world-champion Red Sox.

Answers

1. Rick Miller, who was 16-for-35 in the pinch that year.

2. Charismatic righty Dennis "Oil Can" Boyd, who went 16–10 including the AL East clincher.

3. Spike Owen, whose 46 career homers matched Rice's 1978 total; Rice earned a three-game suspension for shoving Morgan.

4. Tom Brunansky, with just 15 home runs. The team hit 84.

5. First baseman Mo Vaughn, who earned the honor in 1995.

6. Tom "Flash" Gordon, who had a team-record 46 saves that year.

7. Two 20-game winners; Lowe was 21–8, Martinez 20–4.

8. Ring winners in 2004 and '07 include Doug Mirabelli, David Ortiz, Manny Ramirez, Curt Schilling, Mike Timlin, Jason Varitek, Tim Wakefield, and Kevin Youkilis.

"All the time I played, I was always wondering about the person down at Louisville who was going to come up and take my job. You were concerned about that all the time."
—Bobby Doerr, Red Sox second baseman who need not have worried

"Bobby Doerr is one of the very few who played the game hard and retired with no enemies."
—Tommy Henrich, longtime opponent with New York Yankees

HIGHS AND LOWS

For good and for bad, Joe Cronin's name is deeply ingrained in the rich and complex history of the Red Sox. The star shortstop and player-manager of strong Boston teams in the 1930s and early '40s, he was skippering full time by 1946 when he led the Sox to one of their finest seasons ever at 104–50—and within a game of the World Series title. He later served the club as general manager (and the American League as president), but his role in the franchise's failure to move forward with integration is a major blemish on his record.

Already a certified star before coming to Boston, Cronin had been *The Sporting News* MVP in 1930 with the Washington Senators. In his first season as its "Boy Wonder" player-manager, he led Washington to the 1933 AL pennant with his fourth consecutive 100-RBI campaign. His '34 club slid to 66–86, however, and Tom Yawkey was able to snatch him away for the right price: a record $250,000 and shortstop Lyn Lary.

Yawkey surmised that in addition to providing strong play and leadership, this son of Irish immigrants would ingratiate himself with Boston's large Irish Catholic population. He was right: Cronin was extremely popular at Fenway and well liked by his ballplayers, but he struggled to deliver a pennant to Boston. Fellow Hall of Famers including Jimmie Foxx, Ted Williams, and Bobby Doerr suited up for Joe, but another team—usually the Yankees—always grabbed the brass ring.

Cronin's defensive play was slipping by 1939, when he made 32 errors, yet the next summer he orchestrated the sale of stellar minor-league shortstop Harold "Pee Wee" Reese—whom he no doubt saw as a threat to his job. Instead of supporting the Red Sox, Reese wound up helping the Brooklyn Dodgers to seven pennants. It wasn't until Johnny Pesky's arrival in 1942 that Cronin took himself out of the regular lineup for good, and he stayed a key reserve until April 1945.

That same month, three African Americans—Negro Leaguers Jackie Robinson, Sam Jethroe, and Marvin Williams—were given a Fenway tryout to placate those opposed to baseball's color line, but they were quickly sent packing. Both Robinson and Jethroe later emerged as Rookies of the Year with the Dodgers and Boston Braves, respectively. And while the Sox won Cronin a pennant in 1946, his policy as general manager of letting other clubs make inroads at integration relegated his own team to also-ran status by the time he ascended to the AL presidency in 1959.

Stellar Stat: Later in his playing career, Cronin became an extraordinary pinch hitter—hitting an AL record five pinch-homers in 1943 alone.

RED SOX TOTALS (1933–45)											
BA	G	AB	R	H	2B	3B	HR	RBI	SB	OBP	SLG
.300	1,134	3,892	645	1,168	270	44	119	737	31	.386	.484
MAJOR LEAGUE TOTALS (1926–45)											
BA	G	AB	R	H	2B	3B	HR	RBI	SB	OBP	SLG
.301	2,124	7,579	1,233	2,285	515	118	170	1,424	87	.390	.468

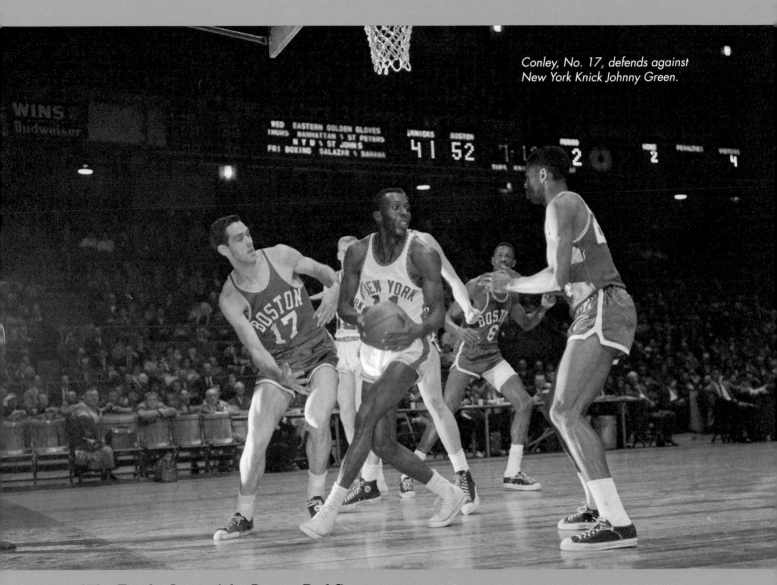

Conley, No. 17, defends against New York Knick Johnny Green.

HARDBALL AND HOOPS

Bill Russell and Carl Yastrzemski were two of the greatest figures in Boston sports history. Only Gene Conley can lay claim to being teammates with both.

The 6′8″ Conley was among the few to play two professional sports, earning three All-Star berths as a right-handed pitcher for the Red Sox, Braves, and Phillies between 1952 to 1963 and spending six off-seasons as a solid reserve for the Knicks and Celtics of the NBA. He captured world championships with the Braves (1957) and the Celts (1959–61), where he often backed up Russell, but his supreme feat may have been going 15–14 for the eighth-place Red Sox in 1962.

DOWN AND SEEMINGLY DONE, SOX SUBMIT A SHOCKER

They couldn't quite deliver a third World Series title in five years, but the 2008 Red Sox gave their fans a postseason comeback as memorable as any seen at Fenway.

After defeating the California Angels of Anaheim in four games during the divisional playoffs, the Sox faced the surprising Tampa Bay Rays in the ALCS. The young Rays—who had never finished close to .500 in their first ten years—had gone 97–65 in the regular season to edge out Boston for both the AL East title and home field advantage for the postseason. Experience, however, favored the defending world champions.

The teams split the first two contests in Florida, but then the Rays shocked the baseball world by trouncing the Sox 9–1 and 13–4 in Games 3 and 4 at Fenway. The Sox had top winner Daisuke Matsuzaka on the mound to stave off elimination at home, but B. J. Upton, Carlos Pena, and Evan Longoria all reached him for homers early in the fifth contest. By

the time normally unflappable Boston closer Jonathan Papelbon gave up two inherited runs in the seventh, it was 7–0 Rays. Some deflated fans were leaving.

That was a decision they would very soon regret. After two out in the bottom of the seventh, Boston scored four times on an RBI single by Dustin Pedroia and a three-run homer by sore-wristed, slumping David Ortiz. Papelbon kept the Rays at bay, and in the eighth the Sox tied it on a two-run homer by J. D. Drew and a two-out, run-scoring single by Coco Crisp.

By the time Drew came up again following an error and an intentional walk with two outs in the ninth, fans could feel history happening; after his liner to right shot over a leaping Gabe Gross, Fenway erupted. The Elias Sports Bureau claimed it was the second-greatest comeback in postseason history. The Sox eventually lost the series in seven games, but they had shown the pride and grit of champions in their Fenway finale.

Kevin Youkilis comes in for the winning run of Game 5.

TONY C: SHOOTING STAR

The consummate hometown hero, Tony Conigliaro went from high school in nearby Lynn, Massachusetts, to Red Sox stardom in just one year. His meteoric rise included 24 home runs as a 1964 rookie and 32 more to lead the American League his sophomore season, despite injuries that limited him to fewer than 140 games in both campaigns. At 20, he was the youngest home-run champ ever.

After the horrific July 1967 beaning that almost killed him, Conigliaro missed that fall's World Series and the entire '68 season. His 1969 comeback was a huge success—starting with a homer on Opening Day—but when his vision deteriorated further after two seasons, he was traded, and then he abruptly retired. Another comeback with the '75 Sox failed, and a 1982 stroke left him severely incapacitated until his death at age 45.

Stellar Stat: When Tony C hit his 100th homer on July 23, 1967, he was the youngest American Leaguer to ever reach that mark. He celebrated by homering again in the same game.

\multicolumn{6}{c}{**PROFILE IN COURAGE**}					
Age	HR	Age	HR	Age	HR
19	24	24	20	29	DNP
20	32	25	36	30	2***
21	28	26	4**		
22	20*	27	DNP		
23	DNP	28	DNP		

*Injured July 18, 1967; missed rest of season

**Retired July 10, 1971; did not play 1972–74

***Sent to minors June 14, 1975; retired August 21, 1975

NOMAAAAH!

There was a time when Nomar Garciaparra owned Boston, when the sweet-swinging, slick-fielding shortstop was the most popular athlete in the city. The Red Sox failed to break through for a championship until the year he was traded, but Nomar's bitter departure in the otherwise magical Red Sox summer of 2004 and his subsequent injury-laden career with other teams should not taint his outstanding early accomplishments.

Garciaparra was a top prospect coming up through the Boston system, but his rookie year—when the wiry-strong, 175-pounder hit .306 with 209 hits, 30 homers, and a record 98 RBI from the leadoff spot—still took everyone by surprise. The right-handed slugger added batting titles in 1999 (.357) and 2000 (.372) and was right around 100 RBI and 200 hits every season. New England Little Leaguers imitated his glove-tugging, helmet-tapping mannerisms, and fans of all ages screamed for "Nomaaaah!" at Fenway.

On defense, the acrobatic Garciaparra earned the nickname "Spiderman" by routinely making diving stops in the hole and nabbing baserunners with laser-like throws. Off the field he was a great spokesman for charities and a model citizen, but a wrist injury cost him most of the 2001 season, and he had a massive batting slump in the '03 playoffs as Boston fell to the Yankees. When Nomar—and the public—learned of Sox general manager Theo Epstein's unsuccessful attempts to snag Rangers shortstop Alex Rodriguez the next winter and then swap a no-longer necessary Nomar, the shortstop was understandably hurt. By mid-2004, with Boston trailing New York in the AL East yet again and a frustrated Garciaparra still struggling to regain his power stroke, Epstein finally dealt away the brooding superstar—a move that, though it helped win a World Series, was sad nonetheless.

Stellar Stat: Before his 2003 troubles, Garciaparra had been a terror in October—a .383 average, 7 homers, and 20 RBI in 14 playoff games.

RED SOX TOTALS (1996–2004)

BA	G	AB	R	H	2B	3B	HR	RBI	SB	OBP	SLG
.323	966	3,968	709	1,281	279	50	178	690	84	.370	.553

MAJOR LEAGUE TOTALS (1996–2009)

BA	G	AB	R	H	2B	3B	HR	RBI	SB	OBP	SLG
.313	1,434	5,586	927	1,747	370	52	229	936	95	.361	.521

STRIKING OUT CANCER: THE JIMMY FUND

Although the Red Sox have gone to great lengths in recent years to blaze new trails after eight decades of Yawkey ownership, there is one area in which they have not wavered: the team's support of the Jimmy Fund.

The charitable arm of the world-renowned Dana-Farber Cancer Institute has been an official cause of the Sox since 1953, when Tom Yawkey picked up the mantle from the departing Boston Braves and their owner Lou Perini (who had helped start the charity five years before). The Jimmy Fund was created to support groundbreaking work by Dr. Sidney Farber into childhood cancer, which in the '50s was still a virtual death sentence. Today, thanks in large part to the fundraising efforts of Sox players from Ted Williams to David Ortiz, the recovery rate for some pediatric cancers is as high as 80–90 percent, and Dana-Farber has grown from a basement laboratory into an expansive research and treatment facility fighting the disease in children and adults.

Dana-Farber's main campus is located less than a mile from Fenway Park, and visits from current and past Red Sox players to young patients in the Jimmy Fund Clinic offer a welcome diversion from treatment. Teenage patients travel to spring training and many games each year to escape the hospital and meet their heroes, and pre-teens get to take their

swings at home plate during the charity's Fantasy Day at Fenway Park fundraiser. The Sox–Jimmy Fund connection starts at the top: Until his 2009 retirement, former Boston second baseman Mike Andrews served as the charity's chairman for more than 30 years.

Special bonds have formed between players such as Andrews and "Jimmy Fund kids" through the years. In April 1993, Sox slugger Mo Vaughn first spoke by phone with 11-year-old Jason Leader and was so inspired by the blastoma patient's courage and baseball passion that he promised to hit a homer for him in that night's game. Vaughn delivered and retrieved the ball for Jason, and the pair stayed pals until Leader's death.

Not every story ends sadly, of course. Uri Berenguer-Ramos had a rare blood disease known as hystocytosis when he came to Dana-Farber at age three from his native Panama, and during 16 years of treatment and relapses, he grew friendly with Red Sox broadcaster Joe Castiglione (another frequent clinic visitor). In high school Berenguer-Ramos started interning in his mentor's Fenway Park radio booth, and by age 21 he was cancer-free and working full-time as a Sox radio "voice" himself with the Spanish Baseball Network. When Uri looked out from his own Fenway booth and saw the Jimmy Fund logo on the Green Monster in left field, he could reflect on the special role the team and Dana-Farber had played in his recovery—and those of so many others, too.

David Ortiz and Amber DaRosa, Jimmy Fund heroes

AGAIN IN 2007

Colorado was the hot team with an 11-game winning streak heading into the '07 World Series, but the Red Sox cooled off the Rockies in a hurry. Starting with Dustin Pedroia's homer leading off the first inning of Game 1, the Sox unleashed a hit barrage—including eight doubles—to cruise to victory. Game 2 was a much closer affair, with 2004 hero Curt Schilling holding the visitors at bay until a double by Mike Lowell drove home the game-winner.

Rookies played a huge role throughout Boston's 2007 postseason, never more so than in Game 3 at Coors Field. Daisuke Matsuzaka started and got the win with help from fel-low first-year hurler Hideki Okajima, while at the top of the batting order freshmen Jacoby Ellsbury and Pedroia went a combined 7-for-10 with 4 RBI. The story of Game 4 was lefty Jon Lester's victory less than a year after lymphoma treatment, and it only seemed fitting that Series MVP Lowell—another cancer survivor—doubled in the clinching run to cap Boston's second fall classic sweep in just four years.

Classic Kernel: Led by Ellsbury's .438 mark, the Red Sox batted .333 as a team—the highest average ever for a World Series winner. Colorado hit .218.

Jason Varitek hits a ground-rule double in Game 1.

ONE MEMORABLE DEBUT

Ask any Red Sox fan over age 50, and they probably still remember where they watched, listened to, or heard about Billy Rohr's first big-league ballgame. Considering the slim left-hander only managed three victories in the majors, that's quite a legacy.

The 21-year-old stepped to the Yankee Stadium mound on April 14, 1967, with Jackie Kennedy in the stands and rookie catcher Russ Gibson playing in *his* first game behind the plate. When, in the top of the ninth, Carl Yastrzemski made a diving catch of Tom Tresh's lead-off smash to deep left, the Yankees were still hitless. And although Elston Howard spoiled the fun by singling on a 3-and-2 pitch with two outs (prompting a chorus of boos from his home crowd), Rohr had unknowingly launched an Impossible Dream for Boston.

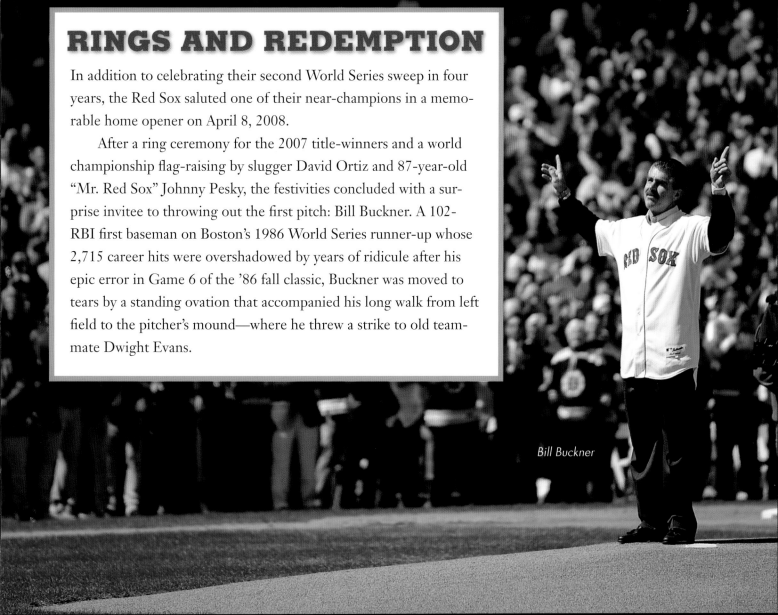

RINGS AND REDEMPTION

In addition to celebrating their second World Series sweep in four years, the Red Sox saluted one of their near-champions in a memorable home opener on April 8, 2008.

After a ring ceremony for the 2007 title-winners and a world championship flag-raising by slugger David Ortiz and 87-year-old "Mr. Red Sox" Johnny Pesky, the festivities concluded with a surprise invitee to throwing out the first pitch: Bill Buckner. A 102-RBI first baseman on Boston's 1986 World Series runner-up whose 2,715 career hits were overshadowed by years of ridicule after his epic error in Game 6 of the '86 fall classic, Buckner was moved to tears by a standing ovation that accompanied his long walk from left field to the pitcher's mound—where he threw a strike to old teammate Dwight Evans.

Bill Buckner

TED SAYS GOOD-BYE IN STYLE

September 28, 1960, was a gray, cool, overcast day in Boston. The seventh-place Red Sox had one more date on their home schedule against the Baltimore Orioles, but it was a game of little importance to either team. Still, the fact that only 10,454 fans showed up at Fenway Park was surprising considering the storyline: Ted Williams was playing his final home contest.

Honored in a short pregame ceremony, Williams took a dig at the sportswriters who had taunted him throughout his career before thanking "the greatest owner in baseball [Tom Yawkey] and the greatest fans in America." When action got under way, Ted walked in his first at-bat and then hit two deep fly balls that were knocked down by the wind for loud outs. He was clearly trying for a last Fenway thrill, but it didn't look like he would get it.

Then, in the eighth inning came a final chance. As the crowd offered him a prolonged standing ovation, Ted dug in against Baltimore's Jack Fischer. He took one pitch low for a ball, swung mightily and missed a second, then appeared to close his eyes as he connected on Fischer's third offering and sent it screaming toward right-center field. As it cleared the bullpen fence, Williams ran out his 521st homer as he did nearly all the others, head down and with no emotion or hand-slapping. He would not come out of the dugout for a curtain call either, for as writer John Updike explained in his poignant essay on the game, "Hub Fans Bid Kid Adieu," "Gods don't answer letters." It was the same thing after the game: Ted quietly left the ballpark to go visit a young cancer patient, and the team announced he would not be going on the club's final three-game road trip to New York. The Kid knew when to quit.

Jim Pagliaroni congratulates Williams after his farewell home run.

INDEX